**DIESES MAGAZIN
ERSCHEINT IM RAHMEN DER
PANORAMA-AUSSTELLUNG „DIE MAUER"
DES KÜNSTLERS YADEGAR ASISI**

*THIS MAGAZINE IS PUBLISHED TO
ACCOMPANY THE PANORAMA
EXHIBITION 'THE WALL' BY THE ARTIST
YADEGAR ASISI*

INHALT
CONTENTS

07 **VORWORT HOPE M. HARRISON**
FOREWORD HOPE M. HARRISON

08 **YADEGAR ASISI: IM SCHATTEN DER MAUER**
YADEGAR ASISI: IN THE SHADE OF THE WALL

10 WARUM ZEIGE ICH MEIN PANORAMA AM CHECKPOINT CHARLIE?
WHY DO I SHOW MY PANORAMA AT CHECKPOINT CHARLIE?

12 ASISI PANOMETER AM CHECKPOINT CHARLIE
ASISI PANOMETER AT CHECKPOINT CHARLIE

14 KARTE MAP: CHECKPOINT CHARLIE / SEBASTIANSTRASSE

16 STANDPUNKT DES BETRACHTERS – SEBASTIANSTRASSE
THE VISITOR'S POINT OF VIEW – SEBASTIANSTRASSE

18 **ENTLANG DER MAUER**
ALONG THE WALL

19 DAS PANORAMA: DIE MAUER
THE PANORAMA: THE WALL

24 KREUZBERG SO36
KREUZBERG SO36

27 GRENZÜBERGANG HEINRICH-HEINE-STRASSE (MORITZPLATZ)
HEINRICH-HEINE-STRASSE BORDER CROSSING (MORITZPLATZ)

27 U-BAHNSTATION MORITZPLATZ
MORITZPLATZ UNDERGROUND RAIL STATION

29 DER TUNNEL IN DER SEBASTIANSTRASSE 82
THE TUNNEL AT SEBASTIANSTRASSE 82

30 WEST- UND OSTBEBAUUNG AN DER GRENZE
BUILDINGS ON THE WESTERN AND EASTERN SIDE OF THE BORDER

32 KÖNIGSKINDER OST/WEST
SO CLOSE YET SO FAR APART

32 MAUERHASEN
WALL RABBITS

34 MAUERGRAFFITI
GRAFFITI ON THE WALL

37 DIE TÜR IN DER MAUER
THE DOOR IN THE WALL

37 WINKEN
WAVING

DEUTSCH ENGLISH

38	RIAS BERLIN RIAS BERLIN	57	ASISI LÄSST DIE MAUER VERSCHWINDEN ASISI MAKES THE WALL DISAPPEAR
38	DER LAUSPRECHERKRIEG THE LOUDSPEAKER WAR	58	ANATOLISCHE ALEVITEN E.V. THE ANATOLIAN ALEVITES
42	JE NACHDEM WIE MAN ES SIEHT: RACHE DES PAPSTES ODER PLUS FÜR DEN SOZIALISMUS DEPENDING ON HOW YOU SEE IT – THE "POPE'S REVENGE" OR A "PLUS SIGN FOR SOCIALISM"!	58	GECEKONDU GECEKONDU
		61	AM TAG ALS „DER REAGAN" KAM ON THE DAY "THE REAGAN" CAME
45	WAGENBURGEN TRAILER SETTLEMENTS	61	KREUZBERGER NÄCHTE SIND LANG KREUZBERG NIGHTS ARE LONG

62 YADEGAR ASISI: MEIN 9. NOVEMBER
YADEGAR ASISI: MY 9TH NOVEMBER

45	KINDERBAUERNHOF CHILDREN'S FARM
46	61 PENNT, 36 BRENNT 61 SNOOZES WHILE 36 BURNS
46	MAIFESTSPIELE MAY DAY CELEBRATIONS
48	„IHR KRIEGT UNS HIER NICHT RAUS! DAS IST UNSER HAUS" "YOU WON'T GET US OUT. THIS IS OUR HOUSE!"
51	HÜBEN UND DRÜBEN OVER HERE AND OVER THERE
53	FASTFOOD OST VERSUS FASTFOOD WEST FASTFOOD OST VERSUS FASTFOOD WEST
54	HENNE HENNE

64	ASISIS FILM DER NACHT ALS DIE MAUER FIEL ASISI'S FILM OF THE NIGHT THE WALL FELL
66	MAUER CHRONOLOGIE WALL CHRONOLOGY
68	DIE MAUER IN ZAHLEN THE WALL IN FIGURES

70 THE MAKING OF

"
WIE KONNTEN DIE MENSCHEN DAMIT LEBEN?

HOW COULD PEOPLE HAVE LIVED WITH THIS?

"

PROF. DR. HOPE M. HARRISON

Es ist kaum noch vorstellbar, dass Berlin 28 Jahre lang durch eine Mauer getrennt war. Auf der Ostberliner Seite waren bewaffnete Posten mit einem tödlichen Schießbefehl stationiert, um zu verhindern, dass jemand unbefugt die Grenze nach Westberlin überquert. Deutsche schossen auf Deutsche. Heute fragen sich junge Menschen und Besucher: „Wie konnte das geschehen? Wie konnten die Menschen damit leben?"

Die Errichtung der Berliner Mauer 1961 und der Fall der Mauer 1989 waren dramatische Ereignisse. Nicht weniger dramatisch ist jedoch die Tatsache, dass die Mauer 28 Jahre lang stand. Dennoch kamen die Menschen irgendwie damit zurecht und gewöhnten sich schließlich daran. Die Mauer war für die Berliner und insbesondere für diejenigen, die direkt neben ihr wohnten, Teil des täglichen Lebens. Genau dies bildet Yadegar Asisi in seinem Mauerpanorama ab.

Das Panorama von Yadegar Asisi stellt für die Kultur des Gedenkens an die Berliner Mauer in der Hauptstadt Deutschlands eine wichtige Ergänzung dar. Die Berliner Mauer wurde zum Symbol des gesamten Kalten Krieges und Menschen aus aller Welt sind davon so fasziniert, dass sie mehr darüber erfahren möchten. Viele haben die dramatischen Bilder vom friedlichen Fall der Mauer am 9. November 1989 und manche auch Bilder von der Abriegelung der Grenze am 13. August 1961 gesehen, jedoch verstehen nur wenige, wie die 28 Jahre dazwischen für die Menschen waren, die in Berlin lebten.

Aus seiner Perspektive als nicht gebürtiger Deutscher, der jedoch lange in Berlin wohnte, ist es für Yadegar Asisi vielleicht einfacher, diese komplizierte Periode der deutschen Geschichte zu porträtieren, als für manche Deutsche, für die die Mauer eine schmerzhafte Erinnerung darstellt. Zum Glück ist die Zeit der Teilung Berlins durch die Mauer vorbei, so dass die jetzigen Besucher bei der Frage, wie das Leben damals war, auf ihre Vorstellungskraft angewiesen sind. Asisis Mauerpanorama hilft uns dabei, uns daran zu erinnern bzw. es uns vorzustellen. Das ist wichtig in einer Gesellschaft, die danach strebt, aus der Vergangenheit zu lernen und die Wiederholung einer so brutalen Situation zu vermeiden.

It is hard to imagine that Berlin was divided by a Wall for 28 years. Armed guards with a shoot-to-kill order were stationed on the East Berlin side of the border to prevent anyone without permission from crossing into West Berlin. Germans shot at Germans. Young people and visitors now wonder: "How could this be? How could people have lived with this?"

The erection of the Berlin Wall in 1961 and the fall of the Wall in 1989 were dramatic events, but the fact that the Wall stood for 28 years is no less dramatic. Yet somehow people lived with it and eventually got used to it. The Wall was a part of everyday life for Berliners, especially those who lived right next to the Wall. This is exactly what Yadegar Asisi depicts in his Wall Panorama.

Asisi's panorama is an important addition to the culture of memory of the Berlin Wall in Germany's capital city. The Berlin Wall became the symbol of the entire Cold War, and people from all over the world are fascinated to learn more about it. Many have seen the dramatic pictures of the peaceful fall of the Wall on 9 November 1989 and some have seen pictures of the sealing off of the border on 13 August 1961, but few people understand what the 28 years in between were like for people living in Berlin.

Asisi's perspective as a non-native German, longtime resident of Berlin perhaps makes it easier for him to portray this complicated period of German history than it is for many Germans to whom the Wall is a painful memory. Happily, the period of Berlin's division by the Wall is over and visitors now can only imagine what life was like then. Asisi's Wall panorama helps us to remember or imagine, and this is important in a society striving to learn from the past and prevent such a brutal situation from occurring again.

Prof. Dr. Hope M. Harrison
George Washington University, Washington, D.C.
Autorin von „Driving the Soviets up the Wall" und „Ulbrichts Mauer"
Author of 'Driving the Soviets up the Wall' and 'Ulbrichts Mauer'

"

IM SCHATTEN DER MAUER

IN THE SHADE OF THE WALL

YADEGAR ASISI

Wer Augenzeuge von Geschichte wird, findet sich später immer wieder in einer Art Erzählerrolle. Oft scheitert man allerdings bei dem Versuch, dem Zuhörenden das – für ihn meist Unglaubliche – nahezubringen. Es fehlen einfach Worte auf der einen oder das Vorstellungsvermögen auf der anderen Seite. Dazu kommt die subjektive Sicht. Was hält man selbst für erzählenswert und was nicht? Wo wird übertrieben, wo etwas weggelassen, wo vertuscht und wo gelogen und manipuliert?

Ich bin in der DDR aufgewachsen. Erst seit 1978 lebte ich in Westberlin. Ich habe beide Seiten kennengelernt, den Osten und den Westen. Nach all meinen Panoramaprojekten lag es nun nahe, auch eins über die Berliner Mauer zu machen. Damit würde ich nach den historischen Stadtansichten von Rom, Dresden und Pergamon und meinen Naturpanoramen EVEREST und AMAZONIEN nun erstmals ein zeitgeschichtliches Thema in diesem besonderen Kunstraum darstellen.

Lange Zeit fehlte mir aber eine Idee für die Umsetzung. Über die Unmenschlichkeit der Mauer wurde und wird in der Stadt viel gesprochen. Als ich mich aber fragte, wie das Lebensgefühl neben diesem Monstrum eigentlich war, erschrak ich geradezu vor meiner Antwort. Es war irgendwie normal geworden. Wir hatten uns arrangiert.

Dieses Panorama beschreibt einen ganz gewöhnlichen Tag im November, irgendwann in den 1980er Jahren. Der Ort ist die Sebastianstraße, einen Steinwurf entfernt vom Grenzübergang Heinrich-Heine-Straße neben dem Moritzplatz. Ich lebte in dem Kiez seit 1985. Die Szenen, die ich darstelle, sind ganz gewöhnliche Augenblicke des Alltagslebens.

Das Panorama zeigt einen Ort, an dem man die Teilung der Stadt besonders gut sichtbar machen kann, weil die Zusammengehörigkeit der Häuser noch sehr gut zu sehen ist. Ein Ort, der so oder ähnlich oft in Berlin zu finden war. Ähnlich dem getrennten Stadtraum am Checkpoint Charlie.

If you have witnessed history, you will later find yourself in a kind of narrator role. But you often fail in your attempt to tell your listener your – often incredible for him – story. There is simply a lack of words on the one side or imagination on the other. What is more, your view is subjective. What do you yourself consider worth telling and what do you not bother with? Where do you exaggerate or omit, where do you conceal, where do you lie and manipulate?

I grew up in the GDR and only lived in West Berlin after 1978. I was familiar with both sides, the East and the West. So, after all my other panorama projects, one on the Berlin Wall seemed an obvious choice. After the historic city views of Rome, Dresden und Pergamon and my nature panoramas EVEREST and AMAZONIA, I would be addressing for the first time a contemporary history topic in this particular art form.

But for a long time, I lacked inspiration for implementation of this concept. There was and is much discussion in the city of the inhumanity of the Berlin Wall. But when I asked myself what the attitude to life was like next to this monstrosity, I was downright horrified by my reply. Life had somehow become normal and we had got used to it.

This Panorama describes a quite ordinary day in November, sometime in the 1980s. The location is Sebastianstraße, a stone's throw away from the Heinrich-Heine-Straße border crossing by Moritzplatz. I lived in this district from 1985. The scenes which I show are very ordinary moments in everyday life.

The Panorama shows a place where the division of the city can be demonstrated particularly well, because it is still very clear that the buildings belong together – a place often found in an identical or similar form in Berlin, like the divided city area at Checkpoint Charlie.

WARUM ZEIGE ICH MEIN PANORAMA AM CHECKPOINT CHARLIE?

Für mich ist er mit seinem besonderen Geist der ideale Ausstellungsort, auch wenn das Panoramabild selbst nicht den Checkpoint zeigt. Als sich die Möglichkeit für eine temporäre Bebauung der Brachfläche zwischen Zimmerstraße und Friedrichstraße abzeichnete, habe ich keine Sekunde gezögert.

Der Checkpoint Charlie in der Friedrichstraße war einer von nur 14 Kontrollpunkten an der Berliner Mauer und verband den Westberliner Bezirk Kreuzberg im amerikanischen Sektor mit dem Ostberliner Bezirk Mitte im sowjetischen Sektor.

Weltbekannt war der Checkpoint Charlie von Anfang an. Beim Bau der Mauer standen sich hier im Oktober 1961 sowjetische und alliierte Panzer mit laufenden Motoren und scharfer Munition kampfbereit gegenüber. Es fehlte nicht viel und an dieser Stelle wäre der Ost-West-Konflikt eskaliert. Auch in den folgenden Jahren war die frostige Atmosphäre des Kalten Krieges an kaum einem anderen Ort so greifbar wie hier. Der Checkpoint war Schauplatz spektakulärer Fluchten aus dem damaligen Ostberlin.

Nach dem Mauerfall hat sich das Areal deutlich verändert. Der Verlauf des sogenannten Todesstreifens ist durch seine heutige Bebauung kaum noch auszumachen. Viele namhafte Architekten haben in der Umgebung beeindruckende Bauten geschaffen. Aber einer der berühmtesten Erinnerungsorte an den Kalten Krieg bietet auch mehr als 22 Jahre nach dem Mauerfall noch immer keinen Anblick, der seiner Bedeutung entspricht. Die unzähligen Menschen, die heute zum ehemaligen Grenzübergang kommen, sollten neben den vielen Eindrücken und Souvenirs auch eine Vorstellung des Lebens und Alltags an und mit der Mauer mitnehmen.

Wenn ich ein Panoramaprojekt angehe, dann beschäftigt mich eine grundlegende Fragestellung und diese motiviert mich dann über den manchmal mühseligen mehrjährigen Arbeitsprozess. Wenn ich mich an das geteilte Berlin erinnere, dann macht mich das Nebeneinander von so Unvorstellbarem und gelebter Normalität bis heute nachdenklich. Das Panorama versteht sich als Beitrag zu diesem Thema mit dem kritischen Blick auf uns und auf mich selbst.

WHY DO I SHOW MY PANORAMA AT CHECKPOINT CHARLIE?

For me, Checkpoint Charlie, with its very particular spirit, is the ideal exhibition venue, even if the Panorama picture itself does not include the Checkpoint. When there appeared to be a possibility of erecting a temporary construction on the waste area between Zimmerstraße and Friedrichstraße, I did not hesitate for a second.

Checkpoint Charlie in Friedrichstraße was one of only 14 control points along the Berlin Wall and connected the West Berlin district of Kreuzberg in the American sector with the East Berlin district of "Mitte" in the Soviet sector.

Checkpoint Charlie was world-famous from the onset. When the Wall was built, Soviet and Allied tanks faced each other here in October 1961, with their engines running and weapons loaded ready for battle. One false move and the conflict between East and West could have escalated. In the years that followed too, there were few places where the frosty atmosphere of the Cold War was as tangible as here. The Checkpoint was the scene of spectacular escapes from what was then East Berlin.

Since the Wall fell, the area around the Checkpoint has changed significantly. With the buildings there today, the course of the so-called "death zone" can hardly be identified now. Many prestigious architects have created impressive buildings in the neighbourhood. But even 22 years after the Wall came down, one of the most famous venues in the Cold War still does not offer a picture that is worthy of its significance. The innumerable people who come to the former border crossing ought to be given, together with the many impressions and souvenirs, an idea of everyday life by and with the Wall.

When I start on a panorama project, I address one basic issue and this then motivates me throughout the sometimes laborious work process lasting several years. When I remember divided Berlin, the co-existence of something so inconceivable with normal everyday life still makes me stop and think today. The Panorama is seen as a contribution to this subject with a critical look at ourselves and at myself.

YADEGAR ASISI, PANORAMAKÜNSTLER

1955 in Wien geboren, verbrachte der persischstämmige Yadegar Asisi seine Kindheit in Halle und Leipzig. Sein Werdegang als Architekt, Maler und Zeichner, den er als Grenzgänger zwischen der DDR an der TU Dresden und der BRD an der HDK in Berlin absolvierte, mündete in den 1990er Jahren in den Kunstraum Panorama. Was 1993 in der Bundeskunsthalle in Bonn begann, hat sich für den leidenschaftlichen Panoramakünstler seitdem zu einem Unternehmen mit etwa 60 Mitarbeitern an den drei Standorten Berlin, Leipzig und Dresden entwickelt.

Seit 2003 bzw. 2006 realisiert Asisi kontinuierlich die weltgrößten Panoramen in den asisi Panometern Leipzig und Dresden. Beide sind denkmalgeschützte ehemalige Gasometer. Eine neue Hängetechnik ermöglicht seit 2011 ein häufigeres Wechseln der Panoramakunstwerke. In Berlin stellte Asisi von Oktober 2011 bis Oktober 2012 in einer temporären Panorama-Rotunde im Ehrenhof des Pergamonmuseums sein Panorama von Pergamon im Jahr 129 n.Chr. aus.

YADEGAR ASISI, PANORAMA ARTIST

Born in Vienna in 1955, Yadegar Asisi is of Persian origin and spent his childhood in Halle and Leipzig. During his career as an architect, painter and graphic artist, he crossed the border from the Dresden Technical University in the GDR to the College of Art in Berlin in West Germany and finally decided on the panorama art form in the 1990s. After beginning in the Bundeskunsthalle in Bonn in 1993, the passionate panorama artist has established an enterprise with some 60 employees at three locations - Berlin, Leipzig and Dresden.

Since 2003 and 2006, respectively, Asisi has regularly mounted the world's largest panoramas in the asisi Panometers in Leipzig and Dresden. Both are former gasometers under preservation order. Since 2011, a new hanging technique has been developed that enables more frequent changes of panorama pictures. In Berlin, Asisi exhibited his Panorama of Pergamon in 129 A.D. in a temporary rotunda in the forecourt of the Pergamon Museum from October 2011 to October 2012.

STANDPUNKT DES BETRACHTERS – SEBASTIANSTRASSE

Der Betrachter des Panoramas befindet sich in der Sebastianstraße auf einem imaginären Baugerüst eines sich in der Sanierung befindlichen Hauses. Hier verläuft die Mauer direkt auf der Straße und somit unmittelbar vor den Hausfassaden. Das Leben fand hier also direkt an der Mauer statt, das mag heute ungewöhnlich klingen, war aber zu jener Zeit ein typisch Westberliner Zustand. Hier in der Sebastianstraße fand ich eine Situation, die möglichst viele Aspekte des Lebens an und mit der Mauer vereint. Zum einen bot der abknickende Mauerverlauf einen idealen Einblick in den Todesstreifen, so war es möglich die Grenzanlagen aus verschiedenen Perspektiven zu zeigen. Zum anderen bot sich das ausgewählte Stück Mauer wegen der vielen historischen Ereignisse und überlieferten Geschichten an, die ich zum Teil auch persönlich miterlebt habe.

Alle im Panorama dargestellten Einzelheiten lassen sich historisch tatsächlich an diesem Stück Mauer verorten. Auch wenn das Gesamtbild fast dokumentarisch wirken mag, sind alle Elemente und Details – wie bei einem Gemälde – bewusst inszeniert und zum Teil überhöht. Wenig von dem, was sich selbstverständlich als Großes Ganzes fügt, konnte ich heute noch an Ort und Stelle so vorfinden.

Das Panorama erhebt nicht den Anspruch auf historische Genauigkeit oder Vollständigkeit, es klagt nicht an, es ist kein Versuch einer gleichberechtigten Aufarbeitung. Dieses Werk soll möglichst viele Gesichtspunkte des Lebens dieser Zeit beschreiben und ich habe die Situation in der Sebastianstraße so umgeformt, dass dem Betrachter das Eintauchen in das Gefühl jener Zeit möglich wird.

Das Panorama zeigt in einem Rundblick den Mauerabschnitt vom ehemaligen Grenzübergang Heinrich-Heine-Straße über die Waldemar-Brücke bis hin zum Oranienplatz. Die linke Hälfte gibt die Situation der Sebastianstraße in den 1960/70er Jahren sehr getreu wieder. In der rechten Bildhälfte aber habe ich an zwei Stellen die den Blick verstellende Bebauung weggelassen, ich habe Gebäude verschlankt oder auch nach vorn verrückt. Nur so wurden die Durchblicke zur St. Michaelskirche, in die Waldemarstraße und zum Oranienplatz möglich.

THE VISITOR'S POINT OF VIEW – SEBASTIANSTRASSE

The visitor to the Panorama is standing in Sebastianstraße on imaginary scaffolding around a house that is being redeveloped. Here the Wall runs directly along the street and so is directly in front of the house facades. This means that life here took place directly by the Wall, which may sound unusual today but was a typical West Berlin situation at the time. Here in Sebastianstraße, I found a location which unites a large number of aspects of life by and with the Wall. Firstly, the bend in the course of the Wall provided an ideal view of the death zone and so it was possible to show the border installations from different perspectives. Secondly, the selected section of the Wall lent itself to portrayal, in view of the many historic events and stories told, some of which I experienced personally myself.

All the details shown in the Panorama can actually be historically assigned to this section of the Wall. Even if the total picture appears almost like a documentary, all the elements and details – like in a painting – have been deliberately staged and sometimes exaggerated. Little of that which naturally fits into the whole picture is still able to be found in place today.

The Panorama makes no claim to being historically exact or complete neither does it represent an accusation or an attempt at a balanced appraisal. It aims to show as many aspects of life at the time as possible and I have transformed the situation in Sebastianstraße to enable visitors to become immersed in the feeling of the era.

In a circular view, the Panorama shows the section of the Wall from the former Heinrich-Heine-Straße border crossing across Waldemar Bridge to Oranienplatz. The left half of the Panorama reflects the situation of Sebastianstraße in the 1960s/1970s very exactly. But in the right half, I have left out buildings that blocked the view in two places. I have slimmed down buildings or moved them forward. Only in this way were the views through to St. Michael's Church, Waldemarstraße and Oranienplatz possible.

Die Mauer in der Sebastianstraße
The Wall in Sebastianstraße

ENTLANG DER MAUER
ALONG THE WALL

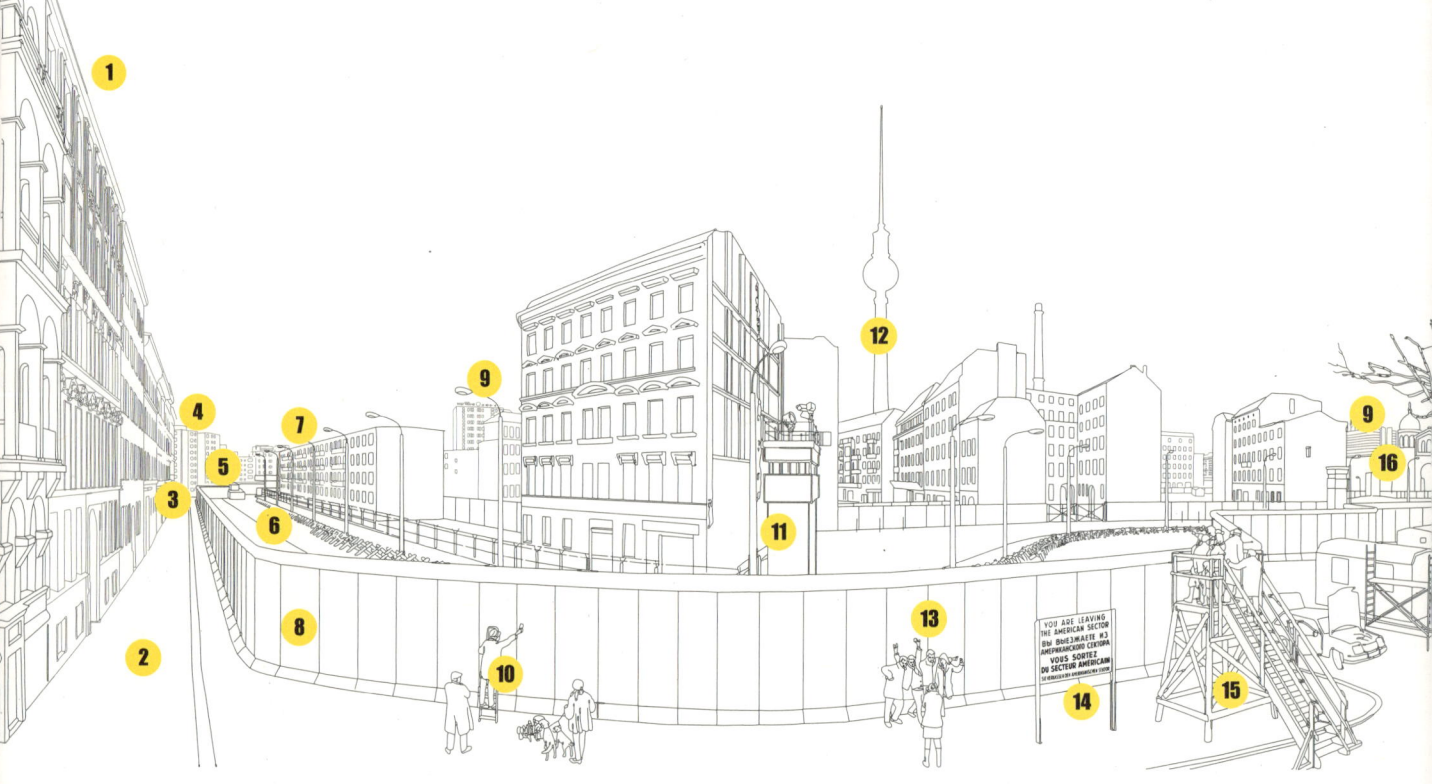

1. Hinter den Häusern: U-Bahnstation Moritzplatz
   Behind the houses: Moritzplatz underground rail station
2. Sebastianstraße
   Sebastianstraße
3. Sebastianstraße 82 (Fluchttunnel)
   Sebastianstraße 82 (Escape tunnel)
4. Westberliner Wohnungsneubauten
   New residential buildings in West Berlin
5. Grenzübergang Heinrich-Heine-Straße
   Heinrich-Heine-Straße border crossing
6. Todesstreifen
   Death zone
7. Grenzneubauten der DDR
   New GDR border buildings
8. Tür in der Mauer
   Door in the Wall
9. Ostberliner-Miethäuser in Plattenbauweise
   GDR panel-construction buildings
10. Graffitikünstler
    Graffiti artists
11. Wachturm der DDR Grenzposten
    Watchtower of the GDR border guards
12. Fernsehturm am Alexanderplatz
    Television tower at Alexanderplatz
13. Mauertouristen
    Tourists at the Wall
14. Warntafel
    Warning sign
15. Aussichtsplattform
    Viewing platform
16. St. Michaelskirche
    St. Michael's Church
17. Streichelzoo
    Petting zoo
18. Teil des Asisi-Mauerbildes von 1986
    Part of Asisi's painting on the wall
19. Wagenburg
    Trailer settlement
20. Besetztes Haus
    Occupied house

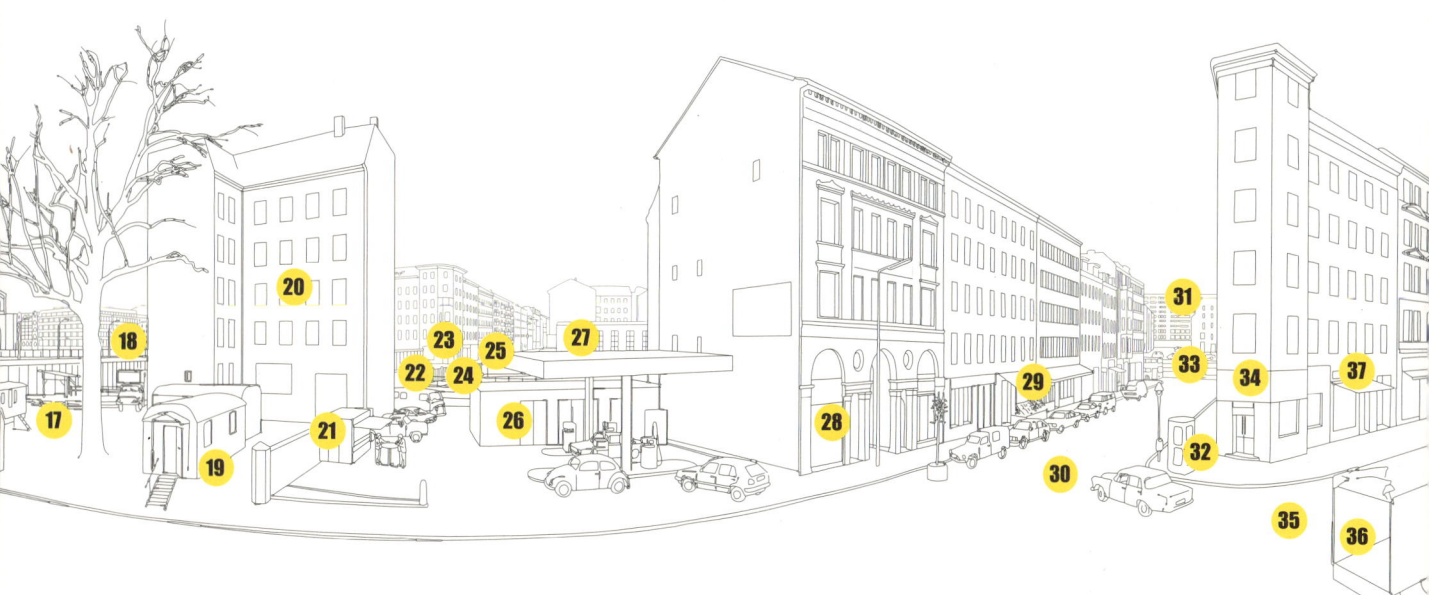

- **21** Currywurstbude
  "Currywurst" stand
- **22** Waldemarbrücke
  Waldemar Bridge
- **23** Altberliner Gasthaus „Henne"
  Old Berlin restaurant „Henne"
- **24** Anderer Teil des Asisi-Mauerbildes von 1986
  Another part of Asisi's painting on the Wall from 1986
- **25** Waldemarstraße
  Waldemarstraße
- **26** Tankstelle
  Petrol station
- **27** Neuapostolische Kirche (Alevitisches Kulturzentrum
  New Apostolic Church (Alevite Culture Centre)
- **28** Kopfbau der (abgerissenen) „Kleinen Markthalle"
  Front part of the (demolished) „Small Market Hall"
- **29** Türkischer Gemüseladen
  Turkish greengrocer
- **30** Dresdener Straße
  Dresdener Straße
- **31** Kreuzberg-Zentrum am Kottbusser Tor
  Kreuzberg Centre at Kottbusser Tor
- **32** Telefonzelle
  Telephone box
- **33** Oranienplatz
  Oranienplatz
- **34** Berliner Eckkneipe
  Berlin corner pub
- **35** Luckauer Straße
  Luckauer Straße
- **36** Umzugswagen
  Removal van
- **37** „Späti" (Spätkauf)
  „Späti" (late-night store)

KREUZBERG SO36

KREUZBERG SO36

Auf der freien Insel Westberlin inmitten des sozialistischen Ostens bildete das im amerikanischen Sektor gelegene Kreuzberg eine in den Osten ragende Landzunge. Ein Teil Berlins, in den sich die Berliner aus den westlicheren und nobleren Stadtteilen selten verirrten. Kreuzberg, obwohl mit etwa 160.000 Einwohnern nur einer der kleineren Stadtteile Berlins, zerfiel in zwei sehr unterschiedliche Kieze, die der Berliner kurz und bündig nach den postalischen Zustellbezirken unterschied: Der ehemalige Bezirksteil SW61, vergleichsweise bürgerlicher und „reicher", wurde vom Ostberliner Stadtteil Mitte durch das Mauerstück vom Checkpoint Charlie bis Grenzübergang Heinrich-Heine-Straße getrennt. Das sich im weiteren Mauerverlauf östlich anschließende SO36 dagegen wurde gleich von drei Seiten in die „DDR-Zange" genommen: Hier verlief die Mauer von der Heinrich-Heine-Straße bis zur Spree, an dieser entlang bis zur Oberbaumbrücke, um dann flussaufwärts wieder zum Schlesischen Tor umzubiegen. Im Süden wurde SO36 zwar nicht durch eine Mauer, aber doch durch eine schwer überwindbare Barriere begrenzt: den Landwehrkanal.

Durch den Mauerbau geriet das ehemalig innerstädtische SO36 in eine völlige Randlage und damit auch ins Abseits. Das Viertel verödete, die Mieten und Grundstückspreise sanken. Trotz der im übrigen Berlin herrschenden Wohnungsnot verloren die Hausbesitzer das Interesse an ihren langsam verfallenden Häusern. Wenn sie es sich leisten konnten, zogen viele der alteingesessenen Kreuzberger weg.

Vor allem die niedrigen Mieten zogen wiederum einkommensschwache Bevölkerungsgruppen an, darunter zahlreiche Gastarbeiter, Erwerbslose, Studenten, Künstler, aber auch eine große Zahl linksgerichteter junger Männer, die nach Berlin kamen, um hier dem westdeutschen Wehrdienst zu entgehen. Fast ein Drittel der rund 160.000 Einwohner Kreuzbergs sind Migranten, meist türkische Gastarbeiter und deren Nachkommen, die hier preiswerten Wohnraum fanden, den es aufgrund der maroden Altbausubstanz und der durch den Ortsteil geplanten Autobahn auch reichlich gab.

Damit wurde SO36 vor allem für Menschen, die andere Lebensvorstellungen und alternative politische Positionen vertraten, ein beliebter Zufluchtsort. Dies ließ eine soziale Vielfalt entstehen, die bis heute die Alternativszene dieses Stadtteiles prägt – und ihn weltbekannt machte. Im Schatten der Mauer entwickelte sich hier eine gewisse Idylle.

On the free island of West Berlin in the midst of the Socialist East, Kreuzberg was located in the American sector and formed a tongue of land projecting into the East – a part of Berlin into which Berliners from the more western and prestigious parts of the city seldom found their way. Kreuzberg, although only one of the smaller parts of the city with some 160,000 residents, was split into two very different districts, which Berliners differentiated very simply by their postal codes. The former neighbourhood SW61, relatively middle-class and "richer", was divided from the East Berlin "Mitte" district by the Wall section running from Checkpoint Charlie to the Heinrich-Heine Straße border crossing. SO36 adjoining to the east along the further route of the Wall was, on the other hand, caught in the grip of the GDR from three sides. Here the Wall ran from Heinrich-Heine Straße to the River Spree, along the latter to Oberbaum Bridge and then turned upriver again to the Schlesische Tor. Although SO36 was not enclosed by a wall on its southern side, there was still a barrier that was difficult to overcome, namely the Landwehr canal.

As a result of the building of the Wall, the former inner-city district of SO36 had gained a completely peripheral location and was now well off the beaten track. The area became desolate and rents and property prices fell. Despite the housing shortage prevalent in the rest of Berlin, property owners lost interest in their buildings, which gradually fell into disrepair. If they could afford it, many of the old-established residents of Kreuzberg moved away.

It was the low rents, in particular, which attracted low-income sections of the population, including numerous "guest workers", jobless, students and artists but also a large number of left-wing young men who came to Berlin to avoid being conscripted into West German military service. Almost one-third of the some 160,000 residents of Kreuzberg are immigrants, mostly Turkish "guest workers" and their descendents, who found inexpensive homes here, of which there were plenty in the dilapidated old buildings and in view of the autobahn that was scheduled to run through the area.

So SO36 became a popular refuge, above all for people with different living concepts and alternative political positions. In this way, a social diversity was created which still dominates the alternative lifestyle in this part of the city today – and has made it world-famous. In the shadow of the Wall, a certain type of idyll developed here.

Sektorenübergang
Heinrich-Heine-Straße
Heinrich-Heine-Straße
sector crossing
1

6
GRENZÜBERGÄNGE
OST- UND WESTBERLIN
BORDER CROSSINGS
EAST AND WEST BERLIN

Stau auf dem Weg Richtung Osten
Congestion on the way to the East
3

GRENZÜBERGANG HEINRICH-HEINE-STRASSE (MORITZPLATZ)

Ausschließlich Bürger der Bundesrepublik Deutschland durften hier nach Ostberlin einreisen. Der Grenzübergang diente außerdem dazu, den Waren- und Postverkehr zwischen Ost- und Westberlin zu kontrollieren, weshalb er flächenmäßig zu den großen Passierstellen an der Mauer gehörte.

Mit einem Lastwagen versuchten am 18. April 1962 drei Männer aus Ostberlin, die Schlagbäume des Kontrollpunktes zu durchbrechen. Von Schüssen der Grenzposten getroffen, gelang es dem Fahrer, Klaus Brüske, den Wagen noch auf Westberliner Gebiet zu steuern. Er selbst erlag unmittelbar seinen Verletzungen, seine beiden Mitfahrer überlebten schwerverletzt.

Um Wiederholungen zu unterbinden, wurde in die Übergangsstelle eine zusätzliche Slalomsperre eingebaut. Dennoch unternahmen am 26. Dezember 1965 zwei Männer aus Westberlin mit zwei Frauen aus Ostberlin einen weiteren Fluchtversuch. Die im Auto versteckten Frauen wurden entdeckt. Grenzsoldaten erschossen den 27jährigen Heinz Schöneberger, der den Wagen gefahren hatte und zu Fuß zu fliehen versuchte. Sein Begleiter aus Westberlin und die beiden Frauen wurden verhaftet.

HEINRICH-HEINE-STRASSE BORDER CROSSING (MORITZPLATZ)

Only citizens of West Germany were permitted to enter East Berlin here. This border crossing was also used for controlling the goods and postal traffic between East and West Berlin, which is why it was one of the large crossing points in terms of space.

On 18 April 1962, three men from East Berlin tried to crash through the boom gates at the crossing in a truck. Although hit by shots fired by the border guards, Klaus Brüske, the driver, succeeded in getting the truck into West Berlin territory. He himself died immediately from his injuries but his two passengers survived although seriously hurt.

To prevent any repetition of such attempts, an additional slalom barrier was installed at the crossing. Nevertheless, two men from West Berlin with two women from East Berlin made another attempt at escape on 26 December 1965. The women were concealed in the car but were discovered. Border guards shot 27-year old Heinz Schöneberger, who had driven the car and tried to flee on foot. His companion from West Berlin and the two women were arrested.

U-BAHNSTATION MORITZPLATZ

Im August 1961 hatte die DDR-Führung auch das Nahverkehrsnetz im gesamten Gebiet Berlins verändert. So wurden einige S- und U-Bahnhöfe außer Betrieb gestellt; Züge, die den nördlichen und den südlichen Teil Westberlins verbanden und dabei das alte, jetzt zu Ostberlin gehörende Stadtzentrum unterqueren, hielten auf den Bahnhöfen im Ostteil der Stadt nicht an. Einzige Ausnahme war der Bahnhof Friedrichstraße, der als Grenzübergangsstelle diente.

Der nahe dem Grenzübergang Heinrich-Heine-Straße gelegene U-Bahnhof Moritzplatz war während des Bestehens der Mauer der letzte Bahnhof der Linie U8 in Westberlin, darauf wiesen entsprechende Ausschilderungen und Lautsprecheransagen hin. Der U-Bahntunnel unter dem Grenzübergang Heinrich-Heine-Straße wurde bewacht. Aus einem kleinen Raum zwischen den Gleisen beobachteten Grenzsoldaten der DDR den Zugverkehr der Westberliner BVG.

MORITZPLATZ UNDERGROUND RAIL STATION

In August 1961, the GDR regime had also made alterations to the local traffic network in the whole of Berlin. A number of local and underground rail stations were closed; trains which connected the northern and southern parts of West Berlin and thus crossed the old city centre which was now part of East Berlin did not stop at the stations in the eastern part of the city. The only exception was the Friedrichstraße station, which served as a border crossing point.

The Moritzplatz underground rail station close to the Heinrich-Heine-Straße crossing point was the last station on the U8 line in West Berlin for as long as the Wall existed and this fact was indicated by signs and loudspeaker announcements. The underground rail tunnel below the Heinrich-Heine-Straße border crossing was guarded. From a small room between the rails, GDR border guards observed the rail traffic of the West Berlin public transport company.

Flucht in den Westen (hier: Köppentunnel)
Escape to the West (here: Köppen tunnel)

THE TUNNEL AT SEBASTIANSTRASSE 82

Siegfried Noffke was born in Berlin in 1939 and grew up in the Soviet sector. In the 1950s, he moved to the western part of the city, where he, a trained mason, worked as a driver. In May 1961, after the birth of his son, he married his girlfriend Hannelore, who lived on the other side of the sector frontier in Prenzlauer Berg. When his wife and child were refused permission to move to the West, which the couple had firmly expected to be granted, and then the border was closed by the building of the Wall only a little later, Siegfried Noffke and two friends, who were facing a similar situation, decided to bring their families from the East to the West through a tunnel. This was an idea which others had too – in 1962, there were successful escapes through more than a dozen tunnels dug underneath the Berlin Wall. But not all attempts to escape were successful, there were repeated arrests and some escapees did not survive.

Noffke and his friends began to dig the tunnel under the border from the cellar of the house at Heinrich-Heine-Straße 48/49. What they did not know is that one of the prospective East Berlin escapees confided in her brother, unaware that he was a Ministry of State Security (Stasi) informer who immediately notified the Stasi district administration in East Berlin. Known as "Informal Collaborator Pankow", he was instructed to express an interest in escaping too and became involved in preparations, without any of the others discovering his double-crossing. When at midday on 28 June 1962, the tunnel broke ground in the cellar of the opposite house in East Berlin, the Stasi were already awaiting the escape helpers there. One of the Stasi men lost his nerve and opened fire immediately upon the tunnel builders appearing from the cellar, although they were not armed. Siegfried Noffke and his friend Dieter H. suffered serious injuries and "Informal Collaborator Pankow" and another Stasi man also received gunshot wounds.

Despite his serious injuries, Siegfried Noffke was questioned on the spot. Only a short time later, while travelling to hospital, the 22-year old father is said to have died of his injuries. His wife and the other escapees from East Berlin were arrested and sentenced to imprisonment of between one and two years for "attempted illegal departure from the GDR". Escapee helper Dieter H. was sentenced to nine years' hard labour for a "state-endangering act of violence" and "inducement to leave the GDR". In the 1990s after the end of the GDR, criminal investigation proceedings were instigated – using the Stasi records kept at the time - against the informer who had betrayed the escape plan (and his sister) but were dropped without any charges being brought due to lack of adequate evidence.

WEST- UND OSTBEBAUUNG AN DER GRENZE

Mit wenigen Ausnahmen wurden die auf der Ostseite unmittelbar an der Grenze stehenden Häuser abgerissen, um Platz für den Todesstreifen zu schaffen. Eine solche Ausnahme sind z.B. die im Panorama zu sehenden DDR-Wohnbauten aus den 1970er Jahren, die nur verlässlichen DDR-Bürgern vorbehalten waren. Ansonsten wurde der Gebietstreifen entlang der Mauer absichtlich verödet. Aber auch auf der Westseite verkamen die Wohnbauten nahe der Mauer. Denn jeder, der es sich leisten konnte, versuchte, möglichst weitab von der bedrohlichen Grenze zu wohnen. Neubauten auf grenznahen Grundstücken (wie man sie in der Verlängerung der Sebastianstraße sieht) waren deshalb eher selten. Ein große, spektakuläre (und auch im Westen umstrittene) Ausnahme war das Axel-Springer-Hochhaus in der damaligen Kochstraße (heute: Rudi-Dutschke-Straße), das der Verleger absichtsvoll im historischen Zeitungsviertel von Berlin, und damit in unmittelbarer Nähe zur Sektorengrenze hatte errichten lassen. In einer Rede an seine Mitarbeiter sagte er, es gelte eine Idee zu verkörpern, „die größer ist, als wir alle es selbst sind. Eine Idee, die heißt: Freiheit für alle Deutschen in einem Vaterlande mit der rechtmäßigen Hauptstadt Berlin und inmitten eines friedlichen Europa!" Als „Schrei gegen den Wind" wollte Springer das 1966 eingeweihte, 19-geschossige und 78 Meter hohe Hochhaus verstanden wissen.

Nicht das Springer-Hochhaus (wie immer wieder fälschlich behauptet), sondern das direkt danebenstehende Gebäude der GSW Immobilien GmbH wurde 1963 vom Westberliner Senat mit einer nach Osten über die Mauer ausgerichtete Presse-Laufschrift ausgerüstet, auf der die Nachrichten der freien Welt nach Ostberlin „ausgestrahlt" wurden. Diese Laufschrift war der DDR ein so großer Dorn im Auge, dass Maßnahmen beraten wurden, diese Laufschrift für DDR-Bürger „unsichtbar" zu machen. Man entschloss sich schließlich ein ganzes Stadtviertel gegen die freie Presse der Kochstraße in Stellung zu bringen, so dass die DDR bis 1968 an der Leipziger Straße etliche 23- bzw. 25-geschossige Hochhäuser (den Komplex Leipziger Straße) baute, um diese Laufschrift zu verdecken.

BUILDINGS ON THE WESTERN AND EASTERN SIDE OF THE BORDER

The buildings directly on the border on the eastern side were demolished to make room for the death zone, with few exceptions, such as, for example, the GDR residential buildings dating from the 1970s which can be seen in the Panorama. They were reserved for reliable citizens of the GDR. Apart from such exceptions, the area along the Wall was deliberately turned into barren wasteland. But, on the western side too, the residential buildings near the Wall also fell into disrepair. This was because anyone who could afford it tried to live as far as possible from the threatening border. So new buildings on property near the border (as seen in the extension of Sebastianstraße) were a rarity. A large-scale and spectacular exception (which was controversial in the West too) was the Axel-Springer tower block in what was then Kochstraße (today Rudi-Dutschke-Straße), which Springer deliberately had built in Berlin's historic newspaper district and thus in the direct vicinity of the Wall. As he said in a speech to his employees, his aim was to embody an idea "which is greater than us all, an idea which is called freedom for all Germans in a fatherland having its proper capital city of Berlin in the midst of a peaceful Europe!" He wanted the tower block - which was opened in 1966, had 19 floors and was 78 metres in height - to be understood as "shouting against the wind".

It was not on the Springer tower block (as is wrongly alleged again and again) but on the directly adjacent building of GSW Immobilien GmbH that a press reader board facing east across the Wall was erected in 1963 by the West Berlin Senate, "broadcasting" the news from the free world to East Berlin. This reader board was such a thorn in the side of the GDR that measures were discussed to make it "invisible" to GDR citizens. It was finally decided that a whole city district was to be positioned against the free press in Kochstraße. As a result, the GDR had, by 1968, built along Leipziger Straße a number of 23- to 25-storey tower blocks (the Leipziger Straße complex) to conceal this board.

Axel-Springer-Haus
Axel-Springer
building
1

AXEL SPRINGER HAUS
AXEL SPRINGER BUILDING
78
METER HOCH
METER HIGH

1968
BAU DER ‚SPRINGERDECKER'
CONSTRUCTION OF THE
"SPRINGER COVER-UPS"

Westliche Propaganda
gegen den Schießbefehl
Western propaganda against
the order to shoot
2

KÖNIGSKINDER OST/WEST

Süleyman aus Westberlin erzählt seine Geschichte mit der Mauer: „Als ich in den 1980er Jahren in die Sebastianstraße zog, konnte der Möbelwagen gar nicht richtig an die Haustür heranfahren, so dicht stand die Mauer. Mit einem Handwagen haben wir die Möbel von der Straßenecke rangeschleppt. Damals war die Straße ganz ruhig und weil die Mauer über drei Meter hoch war, war es in den unteren Stockwerken sehr dunkel. Aber ich wohnte in der 3. Etage und konnte über die Mauer hinweggucken. Das hat mir immer großen Spaß gemacht. Auf der anderen Seite stand auch ein Haus ganz dicht an der Mauer. Von Fenster zu Fenster habe ich so eine hübsche Nachbarin kennengelernt. Wir konnten nicht laut über die Straße rufen, das wäre bemerkt worden. Also haben wir Zettel ins Fenster gehalten und uns dann auf dem Alexanderplatz verabredet. Sechs Monate lang haben wir uns regelmäßig getroffen. Als dann die Mauer fiel, dachte ich, dass wir uns nun einfacher treffen könnten, aber dann habe ich sie leider nicht mehr wiederfinden können. Sie war weg!"

Quelle: http://www.wanderboje.de

SO CLOSE YET SO FAR APART

Süleyman from West Berlin tells his story of the Wall: "When I moved into Sebastianstraße in the 1980s, the furniture removal van couldn't get to the door because the Wall was so close. We transported our furniture from the street corner with a hand cart. The street was very quiet then and the lower floors were very dark because the Wall was more than three metres high. But I lived on the third floor and could look over the Wall, which I always liked doing. On the other side, there was a building very close to the Wall too. And I got to know a pretty neighbour there, from window to window. We couldn't shout across the street, as that would have been noticed. So we held up notes in the window and agreed to meet at Alexanderplatz. We met regularly for six months. When the Wall came down, I thought that we would be able to meet more easily but sadly I wasn't able to find her again. She had gone!"

Source: www.wanderboje.de

MAUERHASEN

In den nur hin und wieder von Postenpatrouillen begangenen, sonst aber menschenleeren Grenzbefestigungen, lebten zahllose Wildkaninchen, die sich hier ungestört vermehren konnten. Dass sie gelegentlich die Selbstschussanlagen auslösten, wie Grenzanwohner immer wieder behaupteten, ist zumindest für die Mauer in Berlin eine Legende, denn hier gab es keine Selbstschussanlagen. – „Mauerhasen" ist auch der Titel eines deutsch-polnischen, vielfach preisgekrönten und für den Oscar nominierten Dokumentarfilmes, der die Teilung Berlins aus der Sicht der Kaninchen zeigt, denen die eigentliche Bedeutung des Todesstreifens verborgen und damit fremd bleibt. Die Tiere gehen davon aus, dass die Mauer zu ihrer Sicherheit gebaut wurde. Für die Kaninchen ist die Teilung eine glückliche Zeit. Waren sie doch im Todesstreifen weitestgehend unberührt und konnten frei von natürlichen Feinden leben. Nach dem Fall der Mauer sind auch die Kaninchen gezwungen, sich im Westen zurechtzufinden.

WALL RABBITS

In the sections of the Wall system only patrolled by guards now and then but otherwise devoid of people, there were innumerable wild rabbits which were able to breed unhindered. People living near the border have repeatedly said that these rabbits sometimes triggered the automatic firing systems, but this can be no more than a legend, at least for the Wall in Berlin, since there were no automatic firing systems there. "Wall rabbits" – Mauerhasen – is also the title of a German-Polish documentary film which has won numerous awards and was nominated for an Oscar. It shows the division of Berlin from the viewpoint of the rabbits, to whom the real significance of the death zone is unknown and thus remains a mystery. They assume that the Wall was built for their safety. For them, the division is a happy time, since they live very largely undisturbed in the death zone and have no natural enemies. After the Wall comes down, the rabbits too are forced to get used to the western way of life.

Zu Beginn des Mauerbaus war Kontakt zu Freunden noch möglich…
When the Wall was first built, contact with friends was still possible…
1

Spuren der Mauerhasen im Todesstreifen
Tracks of the Wall rabbits in the death zone
2

…später nur noch Blickkontakt
…later there was only eye contact
3

MAUERGRAFFITI

Von Anfang an war die Berliner Mauer auf ihrer Westseite auch Träger von Protestparolen: „Ihr Verräter an den Galgen – hier hausen die roten Tyrannen – Ulbrichts KZ-Schergen raus" und ähnliche Parolen wurden mit schwarzer Teerfarbe auf die Mauer und die angrenzenden Hauswände geschrieben. Insbesondere an Orten, an denen es zu Zwischenfällen gekommen war, häuften sich diese Proteste: „Ihr KZ-Mörder"–„In Tyrannis" – „KZ-DDR". Wegen der baulichen Beschaffenheit der Mauer aus gemauerten Einzelsteinen eignete sie sich allerdings nicht besonders gut zur Bemalung oder Beschriftung. Das wurde erst mit der dritten Generation der Grenzbefestigung anders. Sie bestand jetzt aus glatten hellen Betonflächen. Die „Mauer 75" wurde rasch zum „längsten Spruchband der Welt". Nahezu lückenlos war sie mit politischen Parolen, Symbolen, Wortfetzen wie „Anarchie" oder „Peace", „Kilroy was here", unentzifferbaren Kritzeleien, obszönen oder nur dummen Sprüchen überzogen.

Ambitionierte Kunstwerke gab es kaum, Kunstaktionen gar, wie die von Joseph Beuys, der 1964 ironisch „die Erhöhung der Berliner Mauer um fünf Zentimeter zwecks besserer Proportion" forderte, stießen der political correctness wegen auf Ablehnung. Das änderte sich quasi über Nacht, nachdem der amerikanische Bildhauer Jonathan Borowsky (im Rahmen der „Zeitgeist!"-Ausstellung im unmittelbar neben der Mauer gelegenen Martin-Gropius-Bau) seinen „Running Man" monumental über die gesamte Höhe der Mauer pinselte. In den folgenden Jahren nutzten viele – meist anonym gebliebene oder unbekannte – Künstler, aber auch bekannte wie Thierry Noir, Christophe Bouchet, Indiano oder Keith Haring die Berliner Mauer für ihre künstlerischen Projekte. Allerdings waren diese nicht von Dauer, denn meist wurden die Kunstwerke innerhalb von wenigen Tagen oder Wochen von anderen Künstlern übermalt.

Spektakulär waren die Feuer- und Flammenaktionen an der Mauer. Künstler füllten die auf die Mauer hinführenden und von ihr unterbrochenen Schienen der Straßenbahn mit Benzin und zündeten sie an, wodurch Feuerlinien entstanden. Die als Kunstobjekte à la Duchamp an die Mauer installierten Pissoirs oder Waschbecken, die als Kletterhilfen mißverstanden wurden, bauten die DDR-Grenztruppen noch ab, doch den Kampf gegen die Graffitis und die Kunstaktionisten gaben sie nach einiger Zeit entnervt auf.

GRAFFITI ON THE WALL

From the very beginning, the western side of the Berlin Wall was a popular site for protest slogans – "Send you traitors to the gallows – this is where the red tyrants live – out with Ulbricht's concentration camp henchmen" and similar slogans were written on the Wall and neighbouring house walls with black tar paint. These protests were found in particularly large numbers at locations at which incidents had occurred – "You concentration camp murderers" – "In Tyrannis" – "concentration camp GDR". However, the structure of the Wall with individual masonry bricks was not especially suitable for being painted or written on. This did not change until the third generation of the border fortification, which now consisted of smooth and light-coloured concrete surfaces. The "Wall 75" rapidly became the "world's longest banner". Almost without any gaps, it bore political slogans, symbols, individual words like "anarchy" or "peace" or "Kilroy was here", unidentifiable scribblings or obscene or simply stupid remarks.

For reasons of political correctness, any more ambitious works of arts or even art happenings were rejected, such as that of Joseph Beuys, who ironically called for "the Berlin Wall to be made five centimetres taller to improve its proportions" in 1964. This changed over night, so to speak, after American sculptor Jonathan Borowsky (as part of the "Zeitgeist!" exhibition in the Martin-Gropius Building located directly by the Wall) painted his "Running Man" monumentally to cover the full height of the Wall. During the years that followed, many artists, who mostly remained anonymous or unknown but also included famous names such as Thierry Noir, Christophe Bouchet, Indiano or Keith Haring, used the Berlin Wall for their art projects. However, these were not lasting, since they were usually painted over by other artists within no more than a few days or weeks.

One spectacular feature were the "Fire and Flame" operations by the Wall. There were tram lines that led to the Wall and then ended there which artists filled with petrol and lit, so that lines of fire were created. They did dismantle the pissoirs or wash basins installed in front of the Wall as objets d'art à la Duchamp, since they misunderstood them to be climbing supports, but after a while they irritatedly abandoned the battle against graffiti and artists' actions.

> **„HIER HAUSEN DIE ROTEN TYRANNEN**
>
> **HERE LIVE THE RED TYRANTS"**

Mauerkünstler am Bethaniendamm
Wall artists at Bethaniendamm

Familienmitglieder winken aus dem Westen
Families wave from the West
1

2
SCHLÜSSEL WAREN NOTWENDIG ZUM ÖFFNEN DER GRENZTÜR
KEYS WERE REQUIRED TO OPEN THE DOORS IN THE WALL

2

3

DIE TÜR IN DER MAUER

Juristisch gesehen war die Bemalung der Mauer Sachbeschädigung auf fremdem Territorium. Und tatsächlich mussten sich die Künstler sehr vorsehen, von den DDR-Grenzposten nicht überrascht und festgenommen zu werden. Denn es gab überall in der Mauer versteckte Türen, in denen theoretisch die Grenzsoldaten plötzlich auftauchen konnten. Theoretisch – denn praktisch hatte die DDR-Führung, wie sich nach dem Fall der Mauer zeigte, aus Mißtrauen gegen die eigenen – obgleich ideologisch überprüften und für systemtreu befundenen – Grenzer, die Öffnung der Türen sehr erschwert: Wie eine Tresortür waren zum Öffnen der sich nur nach innen öffnenden schwergängigen Grenztür zwei Schlüssel notwendig, die von unterschiedlichen Personen (hohen Offizieren) verwahrt wurden. Waren wirklich einmal Wartungsarbeiten auf der Westseite der Mauer notwendig, so bewachten sich dabei mehrere bewaffnete Grenzsoldaten gegenseitig. Häufig wurden zusätzliche Gitterzäune vor der Mauer aufgestellt, damit den für die Wartung eingesetzten Bauarbeitern keinesfalls eine Flucht Richtung Westen gelingen konnte.

THE DOOR IN THE WALL

In legal terms, the painting of the Wall constituted property damage on foreign territory. And it was true that artists had to be very careful not to be surprised and arrested by GDR border guards, since there were doors concealed everywhere in the Wall through which the border guards could theoretically suddenly appear. Theoretically, since, in actual practice, GDR leadership – as was revealed after the fall of the Wall – had made the opening of the doors very difficult, due to their distrust of their own border soldiers, although they had been monitored from an ideological viewpoint and found to be loyal to the government. Like the door of a safe, two keys were required to open the stiff doors in the Wall, which only swung inwards, and these keys were kept by different people (high-ranking officers). If maintenance work was necessary on the western side of the Wall, several armed border soldiers guarded each other. Additional grid fences were often set up in front of the wall, so that the construction workers assigned to maintenance had no chance of escaping to the West.

WINKEN

Vor allem aus den Anfangszeiten des Mauerbaus sind zahlreiche anrührende Fotos mit winkenden Menschen überliefert, die zeigen, wie groß und emotional die verwandtschaftliche und nachbarschaftliche Verbundenheit der jetzt durch die Mauer getrennten Berliner war. Um diese Verbundenheit aufrecht zu erhalten, ließ der Berliner Senat – nachdem die Mauer eine unüberblickbare Höhe erreicht hatte – an vielen Stellen entlang der Grenze solide Beobachtungsplattformen errichten, die wenigstens den Blickkontakt zwischen hüben und drüben weiterhin ermöglichen sollten. Doch je mehr der Grenzstreifen hinter der Mauer im Ostteil der Stadt durch Hausabrisse und Umsiedlungen entvölkert wurde, desto mehr verloren die Beobachtungsplattformen ihre ursprüngliche Bedeutung. Sie wurden zu Aussichtspunkten für empörte Bürger und mehr oder weniger emotions- und verständnislose Touristen aus dem Westen.

WAVING

From the early days of the Wall, in particular, there are numerous very touching photographs of people waving, showing how close and emotional the family and neighbourhood relations were between the Berliners divided by the Wall. To maintain these relations, the Berlin Senate – after the Wall had grown so high that no-one could look over it – arranged for the erection of solid observation platforms at a large number of locations along the border, designed to at least enable eye contact to continue between East and West. But the more the border strip behind the Wall in the eastern part of the city was depopulated by building demolition and resettlement, the more these observation platforms lost their original significance. They became viewing points for outraged Berliners and tourists with sometimes little emotion and understanding.

RIAS BERLIN

Since the Soviets had stubbornly refused to give the western Allies broadcasting time and decision rights in the Berlin radio station they controlled, the US American military government had founded RIAS (Radio In the American Sector) in 1946. Although reception of this station was systematically disrupted by the other side, the "free voice of the free world" was the most popular station in the whole of Berlin and extensive areas of the Soviet occupation zone because of its magazine programmes tailored to the different population groups and its varied and high-quality cultural broadcasts. In its exceptionally detailed political programmes, it offered not only extensive information on local Berlin events but also placed special emphasis on reporting and commenting on events in the subsequent GDR. At 12 noon every Sunday, the ringing of the Berlin freedom bell from the Schöneberg Town Hall was broadcast first, followed by a reading of the "Pledge of Freedom".

THE LOUDSPEAKER WAR

The GDR reacted with increasing irritation to "provocations from the West". When large and easily legible posters were hung on houses in the West near to the Wall, calling to the border troops "Germans, don't shoot at Germans!", the response from the East was martial Soviet music and loudspeakers with which the GDR regime tried to "inform" West Berliners about the "war plans" and armament endeavours of West Germany.

The West had finally had enough when the visit of the then West German Chancellor Konrad Adenauer to the sector border in 1962 was disrupted by loudspeaker propaganda. At the Brandenburg Gate, he was met with the hit song "There spoke the old chief of Indians…". Thereupon the Berlin Senator of the Interior created a western "loudspeaker service" with the help of journalists from the RIAS radio station. A VW van with oversized loudspeakers drove along the Wall and treated the East to news at various "broadcasting locations". After a blaring initial fanfare, the announcement "Here is the Barbed-Wire Studio" was heard. Then the members of the GDR border troops were asked not to shoot at escapees and subsequently news was read. Every "programme" lasted 15 minutes, after which the van proceeded to the next "broadcasting location". Initially there were four

DER LAUTSPRECHER-KRIEG ENDETE MIT
THE LOUDSPEAKER WAR ENDED WITH
5000 W

Lautsprecherwagen und Propagandaplakat an der Bornholmer Straße
Sound trucks and propaganda poster along Bornholmer Straße
1

Lautsprecherwagen-Kolonne in der Stresemannstraße
Convoy of sound trucks in Stresemannstraße
2

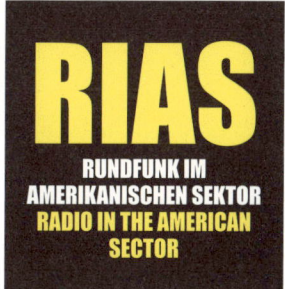

RIAS
RUNDFUNK IM AMERIKANISCHEN SEKTOR
RADIO IN THE AMERICAN SECTOR

Propagandatransparent des Westberliner Senats
Propaganda banner of the West Berlin Senate
3

Propagandaplakat zwischen Mitte und Kreuzberg
Propaganda poster between Mitte and Kreuzberg
4

man weitere Nachrichten. Jede Sendung dauerte 15 Minuten; dann fuhr der Wagen zum nächsten „Sendeplatz". Anfangs waren vier, später sogar mehr Studiowagen im Einsatz. Nach und nach eskalierte der Lautsprecherkrieg an der Grenze: Immer wenn die Grenzer Reporter vom RIAS oder Fotoreporter des Stern, der Berliner Morgenpost oder der B.Z. allzu nah an der Grenze (d.h. schon auf dem Gebiet der DDR) erspähten, flogen Tränen- und Nebelgaspatronen. Die Westberliner Gören, die den Reportern für gewöhnlich im Pulk folgten, warfen diese Patronen gern zurück, zusammen mit Steinen und Abfall, was zu einer wütenden weiteren Kanonade führte.

Der Lautsprecherkrieg endete mit einem grandiosen Finale. Am 7. Oktober 1965, dem Jahrestag der DDR, störte das „Studio am Stacheldraht" die martialische Militärparade mit flotter Musik und eigenen Durchsagen über eine 5000-Watt-Anlage mit einer Verständlichkeitsreichweite von mehr als fünf Kilometern.

Dass danach der Lautsprecherkrieg allmählich abebbte, hatte weniger den Grund, dass – wie auf westlicher Seite behauptet wurde – die DDR einsah, dass sie „den Lautsprecherkrieg wegen technischer Unterlegenheit nicht gewinnen konnte", sondern, weil die phonstarke Westpropaganda auch die Westberliner Anwohner der Mauer traf, die sich massiv über die anhaltende und unerträglich werdende Lärmbelästigung beschwerten.

An die Stelle der Lautsprecheranlagen traten nun Plakate und Diaprojektionen. An etwa 100 Orten entlang der Berliner Mauer wurden große, nach Osten gerichtete Plakatwände aufgestellt, deren Nachrichten alle 14 Tage ausgetauscht wurden. Auf die Erschießung von Flüchtlingen reagierte man sofort mit Sonderplakaten. Ergänzend zu diesen stationären Plakaten gab es mobile Informationswände, die auf VW-Bussen montiert, an der Mauer auf- und abfuhren. Weil die Mitteilungen auf den Plakaten sehr begrenzt waren, ergänzte man diese durch Diaprojektionen. Hierfür fand man unmittelbar an der Mauer etwa 30 geeignete Hauswände, die vom Osten gut einsehbar waren und dafür extra gekalkt wurden. Sobald es dunkel genug war, fuhren Busse an den Hauswänden entlang und projizierten ihre jeweils etwa 15 Minuten lange Diaschau, die meist aus tagesaktuellen Textnachrichten bestanden. Die DDR-Grenzposten waren gehalten, die Meldungen mitzuschreiben. Wenn sie nicht mitkamen, riefen sie schon mal über die Mauer: „Halt, nicht so schnell, wir sind noch nicht soweit".

– and later even more - studio vans in operation. Gradually, the loudspeaker war along the border escalated. Whenever the border troops caught sight of RIAS reporters or photographers from the "Stern" magazine, the Berliner Morgenpost or BZ newspaper too near to the border (i.e. already on GDR territory), tear gas and fog grenades were thrown. The West Berlin kids, of whom a crowd usually followed reporters, took pleasure in throwing back these grenades, together with stones and rubbish, which led to a further angry bombardment from the East.

The loudspeaker war ended with a magnificent finale. On 7 October 1965, the anniversary of the GDR, the "Barbed-Wire Studio" disrupted the military parade with lively popular music and its own announcements, broadcast via a 5000-watt system which could be heard at a distance of more than five kilometres.

After this, the loudspeaker war gradually subsided, due not so much – as alleged by the western side – to the GDR recognising that it "could not win the loudspeaker war because of technical inferiority" but more because the extremely loud western propaganda also affected the West Berliners living near the Wall, who complained bitterly about the continuing and increasingly intolerable noise.

So loudspeaker systems were now replaced by posters and projected slides. At about 100 locations along the Berlin Wall, large poster hoardings facing east were erected, on which new news announcement were posted every 14 days. If escapees had been shot, special posters were hung immediately. In addition to these stationary posters, there were mobile information boards mounted on VW vans which drove up and down along the Wall. Because information on the posters was very limited, it was supplemented by projected slides. To do this, some 30 suitable house walls very easily seen from the East were found directly by the Wall and whitened especially. As soon as it was dark enough, vans drove along the house walls and projected their respective slide shows lasting about 15 minutes and consisting primarily of up-to-the-minute written news. The GDR border guards were requested to copy down the news. If they got left behind, they would sometimes shout "Wait a minute, not so fast, we're not with you yet".

„
**HIER SPRICHT
DAS STUDIO AM
STACHELDRAHT.**

**HERE IS THE
BARBED-WIRE
STUDIO.**
"

JE NACHDEM WIE MAN ES SIEHT: „RACHE DES PAPSTES" ODER „PLUS FÜR DEN SOZIALISMUS"

Die Antwort Ostberlins auf den überall gehörten RIAS sollte der Berliner Fernsehturm werden, der als eine städtebauliche Höhendominante von weithin gesehen werden sollte. Geplant war eine „Stadtkrone, die alles überragt und von der Sieghaftigkeit des Sozialismus kündet". Der Standort wurde so gewählt, dass alle großen Straßen und Sichtachsen des gesamten Berliner Gebietes auf den Fernsehturm zuführen. Ohne Rücksicht auf die Straßenstruktur des dafür planierten Marienviertels wurde der Fernsehturm im historischen Zentrum der Stadt direkt neben der gotischen Marienkirche, in Nachbarschaft zum Roten Rathaus und unmittelbar westlich des Alexanderplatzes errichtet. Zunächst wurde der Bau geheim gehalten, es gab keine offizielle Grundsteinlegung oder Baugenehmigung. Nach vier Jahren Bauzeit wurde der Turm 1969 durch Walter Ulbricht eingeweiht. Der Fernsehturm ist mit 368 Metern noch heute das höchste Bauwerk Deutschlands (und das vierthöchste – nicht abgespannte – Bauwerk Europas). Die Ähnlichkeiten der Fernsehturmkugel zum sowjetischen Satelliten Sputnik, dessen erfolgreiche Weltraummission 1957 der Welt die Überlegenheit des sozialistischen Lagers demonstriert hatte, war durchaus beabsichtigt. Nicht beabsichtigt war das optische Phänomen, das die Berliner Schnauze „Rache des Papstes" taufte: Wenn die Sonne den mit Blechprismen aus rostfreiem Stahl verschalten „Sputnik" anstrahlt, erscheint eine Reflexion in Form eines leuchtenden Kreuzes. Die Aufregung der Genossen war groß, der Architekt wurde deswegen von der Stasi vernommen; man versuchte das reflektierende Kreuz mittels großer Spiegel vom Boden aus zu blenden und so verschwinden zu lassen. In der Volkskammer soll sogar der Abriss des Turmes diskutiert worden sein. Am Ende versuchte man es mit einer Sprachregelung, die das Kreuz einfach in ein „Plus für den Sozialismus!" umdeutete.

DEPENDING ON HOW YOU SEE IT – THE "POPE'S REVENGE" OR A "PLUS SIGN FOR SOCIALISM"!

East Berlin's response to the great popularity of the RIAS radio station was designed to be the Berlin television tower, which was to be visible from afar as a high building dominating the city. The plan was for a "city crown towering over every other building and proclaiming the victory of Socialism". Its location was selected so that all major streets and viewshafts in the whole of the Berlin area led to the television tower. Without considering the street structure of the "Marienviertel" quarter bulldozed for this purpose, the television tower was built at the historic centre of the city directly next to the Gothic St. Mary's Church near the "Red City Hall" and directly to the west of Alexanderplatz. Construction was initially kept secret and there was no official laying of the foundation stone or issue of building approval. After a four-year construction period, the tower was opened in 1969 by Walter Ulbricht. 368 metres tall, the television tower is today still the tallest building in Germany (and the fourth highest – non-braced – building in Europe). The similarity of the television tower globe to the Soviet "Sputnik" satellite, of which the successful space mission had demonstrated the superiority of the Socialist bloc in 1957, was undoubtedly intentional. What was not intentional was the optic phenomenon which Berlin wits soon called the "Pope's Revenge". When the sun shines on the "Sputnik"'s facing of stainless steel prismas, a reflection in the form of a brilliant cross is formed. The East Berlin government was greatly agitated and the architect was questioned by officers from the Ministry of State Security (Stasi). An attempt was made to redirect the reflected cross by means of large mirrors on the ground and thus make it disappear. Allegedly, there was even discussion of demolition of the tower in the Volkskammer (People's Assembly). Finally, the agreed solution was a linguistic ruling which simply interpreted the cross as a "Plus Sign for Socialism".

„Die Rache des Papstes"
"The Pope's Revenge"
1

Symbol des siegreichen Sozialismus...
Symbol of victorious socialism...
2

EINGEWEIHT
INAUGURATED
1969

Walter Ulbricht weiht ein
Walter Ulbricht inaugurates
3

Betonarbeiten am Fernsehturm
Concreting work on the television tower
4

...gebaut unter strenger Geheimhaltung
...built in strict secrecy
5

368
METER HOCH
METERS HIGH

1

2

WAGENBURGEN

In den 1980er Jahren entstanden in Kreuzberg entlang der Mauer die ersten Wagenburgen. Heute gibt es in ganz Berlin über die Stadt verteilt nur noch zwölf Wagenburgen, in denen etwa 600 (meist nicht mehr ganz junge) Aussteiger mit ihren Hunden und Katzen in alten Bau- und Zirkuswagen, ausgedienten LKWs und Bussen in versteckten, idyllisch überwucherten Trümmergrundstücken oder Brachen leben. In der Zeit der Teilung gab es mehr davon, vor allem im Schatten der Mauer fanden sich dazu passende Fluchtorte für die „Rollheimer", wie sie in Berlin genannt werden. Als sich mit dem Fall der Mauer und der Wiedervereinigung die ehemals wertlosen Trümmergrundstücke, die jetzt einen wunderbaren Grünstreifen vor der Tür der aufgelassenen Grenzbefestigungen hatten, als wahre Goldgruben für Spekulanten entpuppten, war es mit der zähneknirschenden Duldung der Wagenburgen und deren Bewohnern vorbei.

Am Ende des Leuschnerdamms befand sich die „gefürchtete" Wagenburg Engelbecken, die im November 1993 von 900 (!) Polizisten gestürmt und gewaltsam aufgelöst wurde. Die Wagen wurden beschlagnahmt und – weil angeblich ohne Besitzer – der städtischen Schrottpresse zugeführt. Während die Aktion seitens der Bewohner, die sich einfach etwas weiter vorrollten, weitestgehend ohne Widerstand über die Bühne ging, haben zwei „Aufrechte" (Angehörige eines Franziskanerordens) passiven Widerstand geleistet, indem sie sich an ein vier Meter hohes Holzkreuz anketteten und den Abbruch der Räumung forderten. Aber selbst der herbeieilende Kardinal Sterzinsky, der seine Solidarität bekundete und bei den Behörden intervenierte, konnte die Staatsmacht nicht aufhalten. Mit Bolzenschneidern wurden die Aktionisten schließlich vom Kreuz geschnitten. In Erinnerung an diese Ereignisse heißt die kaum 200 Meter weiter befindliche, heute noch existierende, Wagenburg neben dem besetzten Georg-Rauch-Haus „Kreuzdorf".

TRAILER SETTLEMENTS

The first trailer settlements grew up along the Wall in Kreuzberg in the 1980s. Today, there are only twelve trailer settlements left, spread throughout Berlin, in which some 600 (mostly no longer very young) drop-outs live with their dogs and cats in old construction site caravans and circus trailers, disused trucks and buses on predominantly concealed and idyllically overgrown derelict sites or waste land. There was a greater number of such settlements during the division of Berlin, and suitable refuges were to be found particularly in the shadow of the Wall for the "Rollheimer" - "rolling homers"-, as they are called in Berlin. After the Wall fell and Germany was reunited, the derelict sites - formerly worthless but now with the wonderful green zone of the abandoned border installations right outside their front doors - turned into real gold mines for speculators, so the former reluctant tolerance of the trailer settlements and their residents came to an end.

At the end of Leuschnerdamm was the "feared" Engelbecken trailer settlement which was stormed and forcibly closed down by 900 (!) police in November 1993. The trailers were confiscated and taken to the city scrap press, since they allegedly had no owners. Whereas the storming very largely met with little resistance from the residents, who simply rolled on a little further, two „upright men" (members of a Franciscan order) put up passive resistance by chaining themselves to a four-metre tall wooden cross and demanding that the clearance of the settlement be stopped. But even the swift arrival of the Cardinal Sterzinsky, who expressed his solidarity and intervened with the authorities, was not able to stop the clearance. The protesters were finally separated from the cross with bolt cutters. In commemoration of these events, the trailer settlement which still exists today barely 200 metres away next to the occupied Georg-Rauch House is called the "Kreuzdorf" – Cross Village.

KINDERBAUERNHOF

Am Mauerplatz (Adalbertstraße/Ecke Bethaniendamm) entstand 1981 als „Initiative von unten" der erste Kinderbauernhof (Streichelzoo) in Berlin. Eine Mutter-Kind-Gruppe, Nachbarn, Kinder und Jugendliche, Menschen unterschiedlicher Nationaliäten und Altersgruppen entmüllten und begrünten ein Trümmergrundstück an der Mauer, bauten Ställe und schafften Tiere an, um vor allem für die Kinder in der Großstadtwüste ein Stück Grün zu schaffen. Über lange Durststrecken hinweg hat sich der kleine Zoo gehalten und weiterentwickelt und besteht noch heute.

CHILDREN'S FARM

On Mauerplatz (Adalbertstraße/corner of Bethaniendamm), the first children's farm (petting zoo) in Berlin was opened as a people's initiative in 1981. A mother-and-child group, neighbours, children, teenagers, people of different nationalities and age groups removed the rubbish from a deserted site by the Wall, sowed grass on it, built stables and bought animals, with the aim of creating a piece of countryside primarily for children in the concrete desert of the city. The little zoo has survived long periods of hardship, has grown and still exists today

61 PENNT, 36 BRENNT

Es war allerdings eine hochpolitische und kämpferische Idylle, denn seine überregionale Bekanntheit seit den 1970er und 1980er Jahren verdankt Kreuzberg-SO36 (im Gegensatz zum friedlichen SW61) vor allem seiner bewegten Geschichte als Zentrum der alternativen und illegalen Hausbesetzerszene.

Die Berliner Stadtplanung verfolgte ab 1966 das Ziel, den vermeintlich aufgegebenen Stadtteil SO36 großflächig abzureißen, um für eine neue Autobahntrasse Platz zu schaffen, über die (nach einer eventuellen Wiedervereinigung) der Verkehr nach Berlin-Mitte fließen sollte. Im Zuge dieser Planungen, die auch vorsahen, den Oranienplatz zu einem Autobahnkreuz mit Zufahrten über den Häusern umzubauen, wurden ganze Straßenzüge entmietet und dem Verfall und der Spekulation preisgegeben.

Nach den Studentenprotesten 1968 begann man sich verstärkt gegen diese Kahlschlagsanierung zu wehren. SO36 wurde zunehmend zum Zentrum der Alternativszene und Schauplatz von Hausbesetzungen. Von den hunderten leerstehenden Häusern wurden zahlreiche in Beschlag genommen, um ihren weiteren Verfall und Abriss zu verhindern. 1980/81 waren mehr als 160 Häuser besetzt. Bei Versuchen, diese polizeilich zu räumen, lieferten sich Hausbesetzer und Polizei zum Teil dramatische Straßenschlachten.

61 SNOOZES WHILE 36 BURNS

However, it was a very political and militant idyll, since Kreuzberg-SO36 (unlike peaceful SW61) owes its national fame since the 1970s and 1980s primarily to its lively history as a centre of the alternative and illegal squatter movement.

From 1966 onwards, Berlin's city planners had the target of demolishing on a large scale the supposedly abandoned district of SO36, to make way for a new autobahn via which traffic was designed to run to Berlin-Mitte (after possible reunification). In the course of these plans, in which the conversion of Oranienplatz into an autobahn intersection with slip roads over the houses was also scheduled, whole streets were vacated and abandoned to disrepair and speculation.

After the student protests in 1968, there was mounting resistance to this wholesale redevelopment. SO36 increasingly became the centre of the alternative movement and the scene of building occupations by squatters. Many of the hundreds of empty buildings were taken over to prevent further deterioration and demolition. In 1980/81, more than 160 buildings were occupied. Police attempts to clear them led to sometimes dramatic street battles between squatters and police.

MAIFESTSPIELE

In der Folge der Hausbesetzungen und Hausräumungen wurde die Auseinandersetzung mit der Polizei geradezu zum Kreuzberger Volkssport. Legendär – und regelmäßig vom Fernsehen übertragen – wurden seit Ende der 1980er Jahre die alljährlichen Ausschreitungen am 1. Mai, die mit Rockmusik, Bier und Tanz auf den Straßen begannen und meist auf dem Oranienplatz mit Krawall, Straßenschlachten, Tränengas und reihenweise eingeschlagener Schaufensterscheiben endeten.

MAY DAY CELEBRATIONS

As a result of the building squats and building clearances, confrontations with the police became something of a popular Kreuzberg activity. From the end of the 1980s, the annual riots on May 1 became legendary – and were regularly shown on television. They began with rock music, beer and dancing in the street and usually ended on Oranienplatz with rioting, street fighting, tear gas and lots of broken shop windows.

Mai-Krawalle in Kreuzberg
May rioting in Kreuzberg
1

SW61
PLZ DES EHER BÜRGERLICHEN TEILS IN KREUZBERG
POST CODE OF RICH PART IN KREUZBERG

Auseinandersetzungen vor besetztem Haus, 1981
Disputes outside occupied house, 1981
2

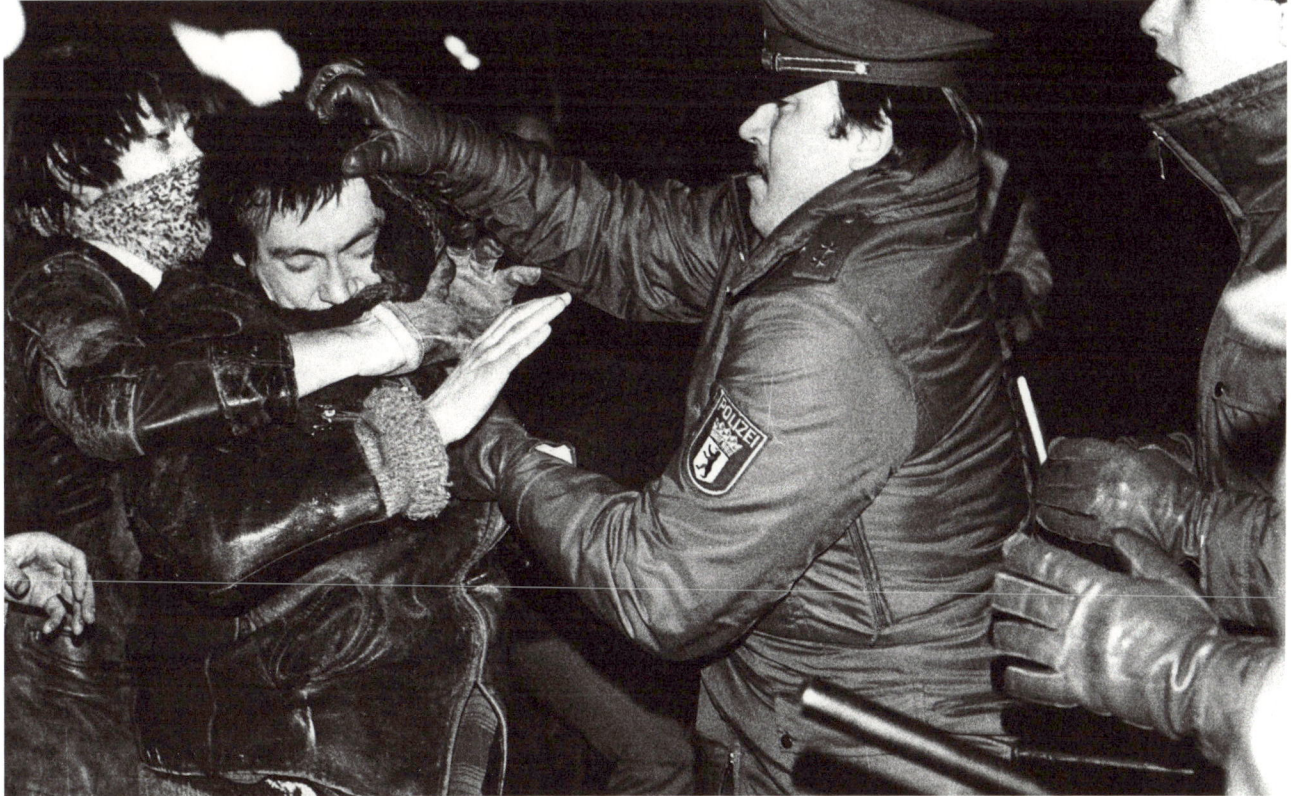

S036
PLZ DES SOZIAL BENACHTEILIGTEN TEILS IN KREUZBERG
POST CODE OF DEPRIVED PART IN KREUZBERG

Brennende Barrikade, 1. Mai 1987
Burning barricade, 1 May 1987
3

"IHR KRIEGT UNS HIER NICHT RAUS! DAS IST UNSER HAUS"

Zwischen den 1970er und den 1990er Jahren waren zeitweise bis zu 160 von Abriss und Spekulation bedrohte Häuser in Berlin besetzt. Das erste in Berlin besetzte Haus war die kleine Fabrik am Mariannenplatz 13, nur wenige hundert Meter von der Grenze entfernt. Ein paar Monate später wurde das gegenüberliegende Schwesternwohnheim des leerstehenden und vom Abriss bedrohten historischen Krankenhauses Bethanien besetzt. Wenige Tage zuvor war bei einem Schusswechsel mit der Polizei der Stadtguerillero Georg von Rauch erschossen worden. Das Haus wurde „Georg-von-Rauch-Haus" benannt. Noch am gleichen Abend rückte die sofort alarmierte Polizei mit einem Großaufgebot an und versuchte die Versammlung von etwa 300 Jugendlichen mit Schlagstöcken und Tränengas aufzulösen. Nachdem dies nicht auf Anhieb gelang, versuchte es der Berliner Senat mit Verhandlungen. Man schloss mit den Besetzern einen vorläufigen Nutzungsvertrag für das Gebäude ab. Etwa vier Monate später versuchte die Polizei in einer Großrazzia mit 600 Beamten, die Besetzer zum Aufgeben zu bringen. 24 Menschen wurden dabei festgenommen.

Unter dem Motto „Keine Macht für Niemand" sang Rio Reiser von der Berliner Politrock-Band „Ton Steine Scherben" jenes Lied, das zur Hausbesetzer Hymne werden sollte: „Der Mariannenplatz war blau, soviel Bullen waren da, und Mensch Meier mußte heulen, das war wohl das Tränengas. Und er fragt irgendeinen: ‚Sag mal, ist hier heut'n Fest?' ‚Sowas ähnliches', sacht einer ‚das Bethanien wird besetzt.' ‚Wird auch Zeit', sachte Mensch Meier, stand ja lange genug leer. Ach, wie schön wär doch das Leben, gäb es keine Pollis mehr. Doch der Einsatzleiter brüllte: ‚Räumt den Mariannenplatz, damit meine Knüppelgarde genug Platz zum Knüppeln hat!' Doch die Leute im besetzen Haus riefen: ‚Ihr kriegt uns hier nicht raus! Das ist unser Haus, schmeißt doch endlich [die Spekulanten] Schmidt und Press und Mosch aus Kreuzberg raus.'" (usw)

Das denkmalgeschützte neugotische Gebäude des ehemaligen Krankenhauses wurde vom Land Berlin gekauft und wird als Künstlerhaus Bethanien und für soziale Einrichtungen genutzt. Außerdem befindet sich in dem Komplex ein Sommer-Freiluftkino und das wegen seiner Küche und seiner Atmosphäre als Geheimtipp geltende Restaurant „Drei Schwestern" (mit Garten). – Das „Georg-von-Rauch-Haus" ist übrigens – nach mehr als 15.000 Tagen – noch immer besetzt. Ansonsten ist es heute am Mariannenplatz eher ruhig und friedlich geworden. Heute leben neben zahlreichen Migranten im Kiez wohlhabende und gebildete Bürger, die für „Gentrifizierung" verantwortlich gemacht werden. Die ehemals omnipräsente linke Szene muss man schon fast suchen, nur alte Graffitis erinnern hier und da noch an die bewegten Zeiten.

"YOU WON'T GET US OUT. THIS IS OUR HOUSE!"

Between the 1970s and 1990s, as many as 160 buildings threatened by demolition and speculation in Berlin were occupied by squatters at various times. The first building to be occupied in Berlin was the small factory at Mariannenplatz 13, only a few hundred metres away from the border. A few months later, the nurses' home opposite was occupied, which was part of the vacated historic Bethanien Hospital threatened with demolition. A few days previously, the city guerillero Georg von Rauch had been shot during an exchange of fire with the police so the building was named the "Georg-von-Rauch House". On the very evening of the occupation, the police, who had been called immediately, arrived in large numbers and attempted to break up the gathering of some 300 young people, using truncheons and tear gas. Since they were not immediately successful, the Berlin Senate then tried to instigate negotiations. A provisional utilisation contract for the building was made with the squatters. Some four months later, the police organised a large-scale razzia with 600 police officers and tried to make the squatters abandon the house. 24 people were arrested.

Taking the motto of "No Power for Nobody", Rio Reiser from the Berlin political rock group "Ton Steine Scherben" sang the song which was to become the squatters' hymn: „Der Mariannenplatz war blau, soviel Bullen waren da, und Mensch Meier mußte heulen, das war wohl das Tränengas. Und er fragt irgendeinen: ‚Sag mal, ist hier heut'n Fest?' ‚Sowas ähnliches', sacht einer ‚das Bethanien wird besetzt.' ‚Wird auch Zeit', sachte Mensch Meier, stand ja lange genug leer. Ach, wie schön wär doch das Leben, gäb es keine Pollis mehr. Doch der Einsatzleiter brüllte: ‚Räumt den Mariannenplatz, damit meine Knüppelgarde genug Platz zum Knüppeln hat!' Doch die Leute im besetzen Haus riefen: ‚Ihr kriegt uns hier nicht raus! Das ist unser Haus, schmeißt doch endlich [property speculators] Schmidt und Press und Mosch aus Kreuzberg raus.'"

The listed Neo-Gothic building of the former hospital was bought by the State of Berlin and is now used as the Bethanien Artists' Centre and for social facilities. In addition, the complex houses a summer open-air cinema and the restaurant "Drei Schwestern" recommended for its cuisine and atmosphere (with a garden). – Incidentally, the "Georg-von-Rauch House" is still occupied by squatters – after more than 15,000 days. But apart from this, Mariannenplatz has now become quiet and peaceful. Today well-to-do and well-educated people live in the district, as well as numerous immigrants, and are considered responsible for the „gentrification". You have to look very hard for the formerly omnipresent left-wing scene and only old graffitis bear witness here and there to the times of protest.

Schutz von Bausubstanz durch Hausbesetzung
Protection of fabric of a building by occupation by squatters

"
GEH DOCH NACH DRÜBEN, WENN ES DIR HIER NICHT PASST!

THEN GO OVER THERE IF YOU DON'T LIKE IT HERE!
"

HÜBEN UND DRÜBEN

Die Mauer hat zwei ständig gebrauchte Redewendungen hervorgebracht, die heute – ein Vierteljahrhundert nach dem Fall der Mauer – von jungen Menschen nur noch dem Wort nach verstanden werden, nicht aber in der Tiefe ihrer einstigen Bedeutung.

Im Osten sagte man – vor allem in den Anfangsjahren der DDR – er oder sie „hat rübergemacht". Gemeint war damit, dass einem Menschen die Flucht in den Westen (rüber / drüben) gelungen war. In späteren Jahren wurde dann mehrheitlich davon gesprochen, dass jemand „abgehauen" ist. Angewendet wurde dieser Begriff, wenn jemand in Folge eines Ausreiseantrages das Land verlassen konnte oder ihm – oft auf abenteuerliche Weise – die Flucht in den Westen gelungen war. Auch boten die Verwandtschaftsbesuche, die nach 1972 möglich wurden, immer wieder eine Gelegenheit zum „Abhauen".

Das Wort „Republikflucht" spielte dagegen im normalen alltäglichen Sprachgebrauch der DDR keine Rolle. Wenn jemand „rübergemacht" oder „abgehauen" ist, so hieß dies vor allem eins: Er hat es geschafft!

Dass sich die Menschen dann oft jahrelang nicht wiedersahen, ist die traurige Seite einer erfolgreichen Flucht. Vielen wurde erst danach bewusst, wie tiefgreifend sich das Leben dadurch veränderte. Trauer, Verlust, Verlassensein – für viele der Zurückgebliebenen waren dies Gefühle, von denen sie annehmen mussten, dass sie ihr Leben lang andauern würden.

Im Westen dagegen brüllte manch aufgebrachter Patriot, dem die Argumente ausgingen, gern „Geh doch nach drüben!", um die ultimative Missbilligung vermeintlich linker Überzeugungen der Söhne und Töchter zum Ausdruck zu bringen. Vielen jungen Menschen waren Atomraketen, Waldsterben, Kraftwerke, Springerpresse und der „Muff von tausend Jahren" unerträglich geworden. „Geh doch nach drüben, wenn es dir hier nicht passt!" Mit der real existierenden DDR aber hatte diese angedrohte Exilierung nicht wirklich etwas zu tun.

OVER HERE AND OVER THERE

The Wall has produced two German idioms which are in constant use but today – a quarter of a century after the Wall came down – only understood by young people in their literal sense and not in the depth of the meaning they once had.

In the East – particular in the early years of the GDR -, it was said that he or she "hat rübergemacht" – "has gone over". This meant that a person had succeeded in escaping to the West. In later years, a majority of people then said that someone had "abgehauen" – "scarpered". This term was used when someone was able to leave the country with an exit permit or had succeeded in escaping to the West, often by a spine-tingling route. The family visits which became possible after 1972 also frequently presented an opportunity to "scarper".

The word "Republikflucht" – Republic defection -, on the other hand, did not play a role in everyday language in the GDR. If someone had "gone over" or "scarpered", this basically meant one thing – he had made it!

The sad aspect of a successful escape was that people often did not meet again for many years. It was only afterwards that many realised how profoundly their lives had changed. Grief, loss, a feeling of being abandoned – for many of those left behind, these were the feelings which they assumed would last for the rest of their lives.

In the West, on the other hand, many an enraged patriot at a loss for arguments took pleasure in shouting "Geh doch nach drüben!" – "Then go over there!" to express their ultimate disapproval of the supposedly left-wing convictions of their sons and daughters. Many young people were finding nuclear missiles, dying forests, power plants, the Springer media and the "thousand years of fustiness" to be intolerable. "Then go over there if you don't like it here!" But this threat of exile did not really have anything to do with the actual GDR.

Ausreiseschild
Departure sign

BROILER WIEGEN ZWISCHEN
BROILERS WEIGH BETWEEN
1000
UND AND
1200
GRAMM GRAMS

DDR-Imbiss
GDR snack bar
2

FASTFOOD OST VERSUS FASTFOOD WEST

Currywurst war das letzte gesamtdeutsche Fastfood. Diese 1949 von Herta Heuwer im britischen Sektor Berlins erfundene und in ihrer Imbissbude im Rotlichtviertel am Stuttgarter Platz angebotene Spezialität war auch im sowjetischen Sektor der Stadt bekannt. Seit 1960 bekam man sie beispielsweise in „Konnopkes Imbiß" unter der Hochbahn-Brücke der Linie U2 in der Schönhauser Allee im Prenzlauer Berg. Mit dem Mauerbau ein Jahr später aber entwickelte sich die deutsche Kulinarik in ganz unterschiedliche Richtungen: „Soljanka", die säuerliche Suppe, die die DDR-Gastronomie aus osteuropäischen Ländern übernommen hatte, kannte im Westen niemand, ebenso wie das „Würzfleisch", das für Westbesucher mit „Ragout fin" übersetzt wurde, mit diesem aber weder geschmacklich noch in der Konsistenz Ähnlichkeit hatte. Während in Westdeutschland die ehemals als „chic" und „nobel" geltenden „Königinnenpastetchen mit Ragout fin" schon in den 70er Jahren gänzlich aus der Mode kamen, steht Würzfleisch im Osten immer noch gerne auf der Speisekarte.

Dafür kannte man im Osten keinen Döner. Dieses türkische – aber in der Türkei gänzlich unbekannte – Imbissgericht wurde buchstäblich im Schatten der Mauer kreiert. Das erste Döner-Kebab im Fladenbrot mit milder Knoblauchsoße, heute das populärste Fastfood in Deutschland, wurde erstmals am 2. März 1971 in einer Imbissbude am Kottbusser Damm ausgegeben. Erfunden hat dieses Gericht Mehmet Aygün, der als 16jähriger aus Giresun am Schwarzen Meer nach Berlin-Kreuzberg gekommen war, um einem Onkel im Imbiss zu helfen. Sein vom Dönergeld gegründetes Restaurant „Hasir" wurde – keine 500 Meter von der Mauer entfernt – das Zentrum von „Klein-Istanbul". Mehmet Aygün starb 2012 in einem Kreuzberger Altenheim; seiner Familie gehört heute die halbe Adalbertstraße. Die trostlose und von Junkies und Trinkern bevölkerte Sackgasse hat sich nach dem Mauerfall zu einem heute meist von jugendlichen Touristen aus aller Welt besuchten Szenespot gemausert.

FAST FOOD EAST VERSUS FAST FOOD WEST

"Currywurst" (a sausage with curry sauce) was the last pan-German fast food. Although it was invented by Herta Heuwer in 1947 in the British sector of Berlin and sold at her snack bar in the red-light district by Stuttgarter Platz, it was also eaten in the Soviet sector of the city. From 1960, it was available, for example, at "Konnopke's Imbiß" under the elevated railway bridge of the U2 line in Schönhauser Allee in Prenzlauer Berg. But when the Wall was built a year later, German culinary specialities developed in quite different directions. "Solyanka", the rather sour soup which the GDR cuisine had taken over from eastern European countries, was unknown in the West, as was "Würzfleisch" (literally "spiced meat"), which was translated for western visitors as "ragout fin" but which had little similarity with the latter as regards either taste or consistency. Whereas the vol-au-vents with ragout fin, once seen as "chic" and "high-class", went quite out of fashion in West Germany as long ago as the Seventies, all sorts of dishes were still served with "Würzfleisch" in eastern Germany.

Doner kebabs were, on the other hand, unknown in the East. This Turkish snack food – which no-one has ever heard of in Turkey – was literally created in the shadow of the Wall. The first doner kebab in pitta bread with a mild garlic sauce, which is today the most popular fast food in Germany, was first sold on 2 March 1971 in a snack bar at Kottbuser Damm. It was invented by Mehmet Aygün, who had come to Berlin-Kreuzberg at the age of 16 from Giresun on the Black Sea to help an uncle in his snack bar. His restaurant with the name of "Hasir", founded with doner money and located less than 500 metres from the Wall, became the centre of "Little Istanbul". Mehmet Aygün died in 2012 in an old people's home in Kreuzberg; today his family owns half of Adalbertstraße. After the Wall came down, this dismal no-through road peopled by drug addicts and drunks grew into a "scene" venue visited today by primarily young tourists from all over the world.

HENNE

Im Westen blieb die Küche kalt, da ging man in den „Wiener Wald". Der Osten dagegen kannte die „Goldbroiler", unter denen sich ein Westbürger nichts vorstellen konnte, weil sie erst im Jahr des Mauerbaus 1961 in Mode kamen. Unter dem vermeintlich englischen Begriff (to broil = grillen) verbargen sich zumeist bulgarische Grillhähnchen.

Für viele Liebhaber galt, dass die allerbesten gegrillten Milchmasthähnchen Gesamt-Berlins, Gesamt-Deutschlands und der ganzen Welt es damals im seit 1900 bestehenden „Altberliner Gasthof" (Henne) direkt neben der Waldemarbrücke gab. Der noch heute existierende Gasthof war immer voll und für seine ortstypisch-unfreundliche Bedienung legendär. Keine fünf Meter von der Kneipentür entfernt und vor den Augen der fassungslosen Besucher des lauschigen Biergartens, wurde damals über die Brücke und entlang des Leuschnerdamms die Mauer hochgezogen. „Habt ihr keine Mütter, Ihr Schweine!", soll der Wirt Conny Litfin die unbeeindruckt bleibenden Ost-Bauarbeiter beschimpft haben. Damit der Leuschnerdamm trotzdem befahrbar und der Gewerbehof am jetzt zugeschütteten Engelbecken für Lastwagen erreichbar blieb und die Patrouillen-Jeeps der US-Militärpolizei an der Mauer fahren konnten, musste der Biergarten weichen. Er wurde gerodet, was den Wirt Conny Litfin so sehr verärgerte, dass er den amerikanischen Präsidenten John F. Kennedy bei seinem Besuch 1963, anlässlich des 15. Jahrestags der Berliner Luftbrücke, zu einem halben Huhn mit Krautsalat einlud, damit dieser die schreiende Ungerechtigkeit selbst in Augenschein nehmen konnte. Kennedy hatte leider keinerZeit, weil er ja seine berühmte Rede „Ich bin ein Berliner" halten musste. Aber da er offenbar von den legendären Hühnern gehört hatte, schickte er einen Dankesbrief mit Bild und Autogramm, der noch heute eingerahmt bei „Henne" zu bewundern ist.

Die Wirtschaft heißt übrigens nicht nach den Hühnern, deren bis heute geheimes Rezept von der Wirtin Rosel Litfin entwickelt wurde, sondern nach dem Ehepaar Henne, den späteren Besitzern.

HENNE

In the West, there was a famous advert, encouraging people to turn off their cookers at home and enjoy a meal in the "Wiener Wald" chain of restaurants specialising in chicken. The East, on the other hand, had chickens called "Goldbroiler", which meant nothing to a person from the West, since they did not come into fashion until 1961, the year in which the Wall was built. The grilled chickens known by this supposedly English name (to broil = to grill) predominantly came from Bulgaria.

For many chicken fanciers the very best milk-fed grilled chicken in the whole of Berlin, the whole of Germany and the whole of the world was served then in the "Altberliner Gasthof" (Henne), founded in 1900 and located directly by the Waldemar Bridge. This restaurant which still exists today was always crowded and renowned for its Berlin-typical unfriendly service. Less than five metres from the restaurant door and before the eyes of the stunned visitors to the pleasant beer garden, the Wall was built across the bridge and along Leuschnerdamm. "Haven't you got a mother, you pigs!" the landlord Conny Litfin is said to have shouted at the eastern construction workers, who took no notice. So that vehicles could still drive along Leuschnerdamm and trucks still had access to the industrial yard by the now filled-in Engelbecken basin, the beer garden had to go. It was completely cleared, which angered the landlord Conny Liftin so much that he invited the American President John F. Kennedy to partake of half a chicken with coleslaw when he visited Berlin in 1963 to commemorate the 15th anniversary of the Berlin airlift, so that the President could see this blatant injustice for himself. Sadly, Kennedy did not have the time, because he had to give his famous "Ich bin ein Berliner" speech. But since he had apparently heard of the legendary chicken, he sent a letter of thanks with a picture and an autograph, which was framed and can still be admired in the "Henne" (German for hen) today.

Incidentally, the restaurant is not called after the chicken, for which the recipe, still kept secret today, was developed by the landlady Rosel Litfin, but after the subsequent owners, Mr. and Mrs. Henne.

Blick auf den Leuschnerdamm
View of Leuschnerdamm
1

DEN ALTBERLINER
GASTHOF GIBT ES SEIT
THE OLD BERLIN PUB HAS
BEEN EXISTING SINCE
1900

2

Yadegar Asisi in den 1980er Jahren
Yadegar Asisi in the 1980s
2

Durch Asisis Illusionsmalerei scheint
die Mauer verschwunden
Through Asisi's "tromp d'oeil" painting,
the Wall seems to have disappeared
1

Die Mauer am Oranienplatz
vor der Bemalung
The Wall at Oranienplatz
before it was painted
3

ASISI LÄSST DIE MAUER VERSCHWINDEN
ASISI MAKES THE WALL DISAPPEAR

Folgt man in östlicher Richtung der Sebastianstraße, führt der Weg entlang der Mauermarkierung durch die Luckauer Straße zur Waldemarstraße. Sie überquert den zugeschütteten Luisenstädtischen Kanal, der bis 1989 Teil der Grenzanlagen war.

Mit dem Bau der Berliner Mauer wurde auch der auf die Sankt-Michaels-Kirche zuführende ehemalige Luisenstädtische Kanal, jetzt Parkanlage, in eine Grenzsperranlage umgewandelt und das Engelbecken vor der Kirche zugeschüttet. Von der Kirche, die im Ostteil der Stadt lag, war von Westberlin aus, wo die meisten Gemeindemitglieder lebten, nur noch die obere Hälfte mit dem Turm zu sehen.

1986 ließ Yadegar Asisi durch eine Illusionsmalerei die Mauer „verschwinden", und fast schien es so, als könne man, wie früher, wieder geradewegs auf die Kirche zugehen. Asisi projizierte auf die nach Westen gerichtete Mauerseite den durch die Mauer versperrten Blick und rekonstruierte mit Pinsel und Farbe den Zustand des vor dem Mauerbau belebten Engelbeckens.

Später kamen die Akteure des „Weißen Strichs", junge, aus der DDR ausgereiste Künstler, die mit ihrer Kunstaktion gegen die Gewöhnung an die Mauer in Westberlin protestierten. Als Akt der „Re-Visualisierung" zogen sie ihren weißen Strich auch mitten durch Asisis Gemälde und zerstörten damit das Illusionsbild.

Als die Mauer im November 1989 fiel und wenig später abgebaut wurde, blieb eines der beiden Segmente, auf denen Yadegar Asisi sein Kunstwerk gemalt hatte, erhalten. Auf einer Auktion in Monaco ersteigerte der italienische Geschäftsmann Marco Piccinini das 2,6 Tonnen schwere Betonsegment und machte es wegen seiner geschichtsträchtigen Bemalung Papst Johannes Paul II. zum Geschenk. Seit Herbst 1990 ist das Mauerstück in den Vatikanischen Gärten aufgestellt.

If you follow Sebastianstraße in an eastern direction, your route takes you along the marked course of the Wall through Luckauerstraße to Waldemarstraße. It crosses the filled-in Luisenstädtische Canal, which was part of the border installations until 1989.

When the Berlin Wall was built, the former Luisenstädtische Canal leading to St. Michael's Church was also turned into a border barrier and the Engelbecken basin outside the church was filled in. From West Berlin, where most of the members of the congregation of St. Michael's Church lived, only the upper part of the church with the spire could be seen, since it was now in the eastern part of the city.

With an illusionist painting, Yadegar Asisi made the Wall "disappear" in 1986 and it almost looked as if you could walk straight to the church as in the past. Asisi projected the view blocked by the Wall onto the western side of the Wall and reconstructed the Engelbecken basin, which had been a hive of activity before the Wall was built.

Later, there came young artists who had left the GDR and formed the "White Streak". They protested with their art programmes against people becoming accustomed to the Wall in West Berlin. As an act of "revisualisation", they also drew their white streak right through Asisi's work and thus destroyed the illusionist painting.

When the Wall fell in November 1989 and was dismantled shortly afterwards, one of the segments on which Yadegar Asisi had done his painting was able to be rescued. At an auction in Monaco, the Italian businessman Marco Piccinini bought the concrete segment weighing 2.6 tonnes and gave it to Pope John Paul II in view of its historic significance. This piece of the Berlin Wall has stood in the Vatican Gardens since 1990.

Mauersegment mit Asisis Bemalung in den Vatikanischen Gärten
Wall segment with Asisi's painting in the Vatican Gardens
4

ANATOLISCHE ALEVITEN E.V.

Gegenüber der „Henne", auf der anderen Seite der Waldemarstraße, die zu einem hohen Prozentsatz von Türken bewohnt wird, lag die 1957 errichtete Neuapostolische Kirche, ein Neubau von praktischer Hässlichkeit. Die Umwidmung dieser Kirche 1999 in ein Cemevi – einem Gebetsraum und ein Kulturzentrum der in der Türkei nicht anerkannten Anatolischen Aleviten mit 1400 Gemeindemitgliedern in Kreuzberg – markiert einmal mehr die Umwandlung des Kiezes in ein multikulturelles „Klein-Instanbul". Eigentlich müsste es aber „Klein-Erzurum" heißen, denn die etwa hundert Großfamilien in dieser Straße stammen alle aus dem ostanatolischen Dorf Kelkit. Die nächste Großstadt ist Erzurum.

GECEKONDU

Auf Türkisch heißen illegale Siedlungen Gecekondu (über Nacht hingestellt). Berlins einziges Gecekondu verdankt sich der Mauer: Unmittelbar neben der direkt an der Mauer gelegenen Thomaskirche lag spitzwinklig ein knapp 500 Quadratmeter großes Stück Land auf dem Gebiet des Ostsektors so ungünstig, dass die DDR beim Bau der Grenzbefestigung darauf verzichtete, es in den Mauerverlauf einzubeziehen. Dass diese DDR-Exklave nutzlos vor sich hin verwilderte, konnte Osman Kalin nicht verstehen. Er befreite das Land von Müll und Unrat, pflanzte Kohl und Sonnenblumen. Plötzlich war der Garten umzäunt, und eines Tages stand da fast „über Nacht" ein Gartenhäuschen, aus alten Baubalken und Sperrholzplatten zusammengenagelt, Wein umrankt und hielt das zweistöckige Gebäude mit winzigem Balkon zusammen. Birnen-, Pflaumen- und sogar ein Aprikosenbaum gehörten zur Idylle ebenso wie mannshohe Bohnen- und Tomatenstauden. Doch eines Tages standen sie da! Zwei bewaffnete Soldaten des Grenzregiments Nr. 33 krochen durch die „geheime" Mauertür und fragten: „‚Was machst Du? Wem gehört das Land?' Ich habe gesagt: ‚Mir!' Sie haben gesagt: ‚Gehört nicht dir, gehört der DDR!' Ich habe gesagt: ‚Geht nicht, ich schon so lange hier.'" Als der Türke überhaupt nicht und nichts verstand (oder verstehen wollte), resignierten die Grenzer: „Sie haben gesagt: ‚In Ordnung! Machst du Garten' ..." Was hätten sie auch sonst tun können?!

Doch nichts bleibt, wie es ist – schon gar nicht die Idylle. Als Kalin alt wurde und die Gartenarbeit beschwerlich, gab er ein Stück Land an einen Nachbarn ab. Eine Zeitlang ackerten die beiden Landsmänner in friedlicher Koexistenz, dann aber kam es zum Streit, zu Schlägerei und schließlich zu einem heftigen Nachbarschaftskrieg. Ein Maschendrahtzaun wurde gezogen, der heute die Niemandsland-Idylle in einen Ost- und einen Westteil trennt!

THE ANATOLIAN ALEVITES

Opposite the "Henne", on the other side of Waldemarstraße, of which many of the residents are Turkish, is the New Apostolic Church built in 1957, a new building of practical ugliness. The rededication of this church in 1999 as a "cemevi" – a prayer room and a culture centre for the Anatolian Alevites who are not recognised in Turkey and have 1400 members in Kreuzberg – is another indication of the conversion of the district into a multicultural "Little Istanbul". Actually, it should be called "Little Erzurum", since the approximately hundred extended families in this street all come from the village of Kelkit in East Anatolia. The next large town is Erzurum.

GECEKONDU

In Turkish, illegal settlements are called "gecekondu" (built overnight). Berlin's only original gecekondu is a direct result of the Wall. Right by St. Thomas' Church which was situated directly by the Wall, there was an acute-angled piece of land just under 500 square metres in size. It was located so awkwardly on the territory of the eastern sector that the GDR did not include it in the Wall when the latter was built. Osman Kalin could not understand why this GDR exclave was left to uselessly run wild. He cleared it of rubbish and waste, planted cabbage and sunflowers. Suddenly the garden had a fence and one day a "summerhouse" appeared almost "overnight", nailed recklessly together from old construction timber and plywood boards, entwined by vines, the two-storey building is held together by a tiny balcony. This idyll includes a pear tree, a plum tree and even an apricot tree, together with man-sized bean and tomato plants. But one day they came! Two soldiers from the No. 33 Border Regiment crawled through the "secret" Wall door and asked: "‚What are you doing? Who does the land belong to?' I said: ‚Me!' They said: ‚It doesn't belong to you, it belongs to the GDR!' I said: ‚Not true, I been here so long.'" When the Turk failed to understand what they were trying to say (or refused to understand them), the border guards gave up and left. "They said: ‚All right! Do your garden'..." What else could they have done?!

But nothing remains unchanged, not even such an idyll. As Kalin grew old and gardening became difficult for him, he gave a piece of land to a neighbour. For a while, the two fellow countrymen worked peacefully together, but then there was an argument, a fight and finally a serious neighbourhood war. A wire-mesh fence was put up, which today divides the no man's land into an eastern and western part!

Gecekondu – Eine grüne
Oase an der Mauer
Gecekondu – a green
oasis by the Wall
1

Bis heute besetzt:
Berlins einziger Gecekondu
Still occupied today:
Berlin's only Gecekondu
2

500QM
GROSS IST DAS STÜCK LAND
AUF DEM MAUERSTREIFEN
BIG IS THE PIECE OF LAND ON
THE STRIP OF THE WALL

75%
TÜRKISCHER ABSTAMMUNG
LEBEN IN WALDEMARSTRASSE
POST CODE OF RICH PART
IN KREUZBERG

Türkischer Einwanderer im
Berlin der 1970er Jahre
Turkish immigrants in Berlin
in the 1970s
3

REAGAN BESUCHTE BERLIN AM
REAGAN VISITED BERLIN ON THE
17. JULI
1987

Ronald Reagan am Checkpoint Charlie
Ronald Reagon at Checkpoint Charlie
1

S036
WAR ABGERIEGELT, NIEMAND KAM REIN ODER RAUS
WAS SEALED OFF, NO-ONE COULD ENTER OR LEAVE

Polizeikette in Kreuzberg, Juni 1987
Police chain in Kreuzberg, June 1987
2

AM TAG ALS „DER REAGAN" KAM

Als bekannt wurde, dass US-Präsident Ronald Reagan zu einer zehnstündigen Stippvisite nach Berlin kommen würde, schallte aus den weitgeöffneten Fenstern der besetzten Häuser in Kreuzberg dröhnend der gerade aktuelle Schlager „Am Tag, als der Regen kam, langersehnt …". Von der Staatsmacht wurde das als Drohung verstanden. Die Furcht vor den Kreuzberger Alternativen und Krawallmachern war so groß, dass am Tag des Staatsbesuches der gesamte Stadtteil Kreuzbergs abgeriegelt wurde. Nach SO36 kam keiner mehr hinein und keiner heraus. U-Bahnen, Busse, Autos wurden gestoppt und noch bis spät in die Nacht an der Weiterfahrt gehindert. Kinder konnten nicht zu ihren Eltern, Eltern suchten vergeblich ihre Kinder, wichtige Transporte mit Lebensmitteln oder Medikamenten blieben unerledigt. Dieses Vorgehen wurde von den Kreuzberger Alternativen durch die Forderung nach einer Mauer um ganz Kreuzberg ironisiert. Damit brachte man Polizei und Anwohner in Verlegenheit: Am 17. Juni 1987 sperrte ihr „Büro für ungewöhnliche Maßnahmen" den Stadtteil durch eine blitzartig errichtete Mauer am Kottbusser Damm ab. Die Brücke über den Landwehrkanal und das dahinter liegende „Freiwildgelände SO36" konnte nur noch mit angeblich vom Berliner Senat ausgegebenen Passierscheinen betreten werden.

ON THE DAY "THE REAGAN" CAME

When it was announced that US President Ronald Reagan was coming on a ten-hour whirlwind trip to Berlin, the then popular hit song "On the day when the rains came, long-awaited…." (The German word for "rains" is "Regen"!) was heard playing loudly from the wide-open windows of the occupied houses in Kreuzberg. The government saw this as a threat. Their fear of the Kreuzberg alternative movement and rowdies was so great that the whole district of Kreuzberg was sealed off on the day of the state visit. No-one could enter or leave SO36. Underground railway trains, buses and cars were stopped and prevented from continuing until late at night. Children could not get to their parents and parents looked for their children in vain; important food and medicines were not able to be delivered. This procedure was mocked by the Kreuzberg alternative movement by calling for a wall right round Kreuzberg. Both police and residents were put in a tight spot – on 17 June 1987, the "Bureau for Unusual Measures" closed off the city district with a wall built at lightning speed at Kottbuser Damm. The bridge over the Landwehr canal and the "SO36 Game Reserve" behind it could only be accessed with passes alleged issued by the Berlin Senate.

KREUZBERGER NÄCHTE SIND LANG

Trotz der oftmals politisch aufgeladenen und kämpferischen Atmosphäre (bierernst ging es dabei nicht wirklich zu): Die legendäre Kreuzberger Kneipenszene wurde 1978 durch den „Blödel-Song" der Gebrüder Blattschuss besungen, der mehrere Wochen lang die deutschen Charts beherrschte und nicht wenig zum Kneipentourismus in SO36 beitrug.

> Jetzt fragt mich doch so'n Typ ob ich studier', ich sag':
> „ja, Wirtschaftspolitik, d'rum sitz ich hier". Da sagt er, daß er von der Zeitung wär', und da wär' er der Lokalredakteur. Ein Rentner ruft: „ihr solltet euch was schäm'!",
> ein andrer meint, das läge am System. Das ist so krank wie meine Leber, sag ich barsch, die zwölf Semester waren doch nicht so janz umsonst.
>
> Kreuzberger Nächte sind lang,
> Kreuzberger Nächte sind lang,
> erst fang'se janz langsam an,
> aber dann, aber dann!

KREUZBERG NIGHTS ARE LONG

Despite the frequently politically charged and militant atmosphere (things were never really deadly serious), the legendary Kreuzberg pub scene was extolled in a „Blödel-Song" (nonsense song) by the Blattschuss brothers in 1978. It dominated the German charts for several weeks and undoubtedly made a considerable contribution to pub tourism in SO36.

YADEGAR ASISI

Fast Dreiundzwanzig Jahre ist er nun her – dieser Tag im November 1989, der Tag, an dem die Mauer fiel. Wie wohl viele andere, erinnere ich mich heute noch sehr genau daran, wie ich diesen Tag damals erlebte: Ich arbeitete in meinem Atelier. Freunde, die zu Besuch waren, schalteten den Fernsehapparat ein und fingen plötzlich laut zu schreien an: „Die Mauer ist weg! Die Mauer ist weg!"

Reflexartig rannten wir auf die Straße, sprangen in meinen Renault-Kastenwagen und fuhren mit lautem Getöse in Richtung Grenze. Erste Station war die Oberbaumbrücke in Kreuzberg. Sie war geschlossen. Hier war kein Durchkommen. Danach fuhren wir zum Moritzplatz, Grenzübergang Heinestraße. Und hier war die Grenze irgendwie geöffnet und doch zu. Ein seltsames Bild; bis heute kann ich es kaum glauben: Wir spielten „Hasch mich" mit den Grenzern. Wir täuschten links an, um rechts durch die Grenze durchzurennen. Und dann dasselbe von rechts. Irgendwann gaben wir uns geschlagen. Die Grenzer hatten noch einmal gewonnen. Aber wir wollten unbedingt in den Osten Berlins – sofort. Also war jetzt das Ziel aller Ziele das Brandenburger Tor. Auf der Mauer standen zahllose Menschen. Mir war bis dahin nicht klar gewesen, dass hier die Mauerkrone so breit war, dass so viele Menschen dort Platz fanden. Auch wir kletterten hinauf und überlegten, ob wir auf die Ostseite hinunterspringen sollten. Ein Freund aus unserer Gruppe war fünf Tage zuvor noch aus einem Gefängnis in der DDR in den Westen abgeschoben worden. Er schrie laut: „Ich komme doch gerade von dort, jetzt soll ich wieder hin!?" Aber wie wir alle, ließ auch er sich fallen. Jetzt stand ich nur wenige Meter vom Brandenburger Tor entfernt. Ein Polizist kam geradewegs auf mich zu und fragte im besten Sächsisch: „Wo wolln sien hin?". Ich war sprachlos. Er kam näher: „Wolln si in de Haubdstadt?". Ich sagte einfach „Ja!" – und der Weg in die „Haubdstadt" war frei. Es war wie in einem Rausch, allerdings ganz ohne Alkohol. Es war ein Gefühl größter Überwältigung, ein Gefühl größter Freude.

Alles was später an Feierlichkeiten und Festen noch kam, hatte für mich nicht annähernd mehr die Kraft dieses Augenblicks: Der Abend des 9. Novembers 1989 unter dem Brandenburger Tor ....

Almost twenty-three years have now passed since that day in November 1989, the day when the Wall came down. Like many other people, I still remember very clearly how I spent that day. I was working in my studio. Friends who were visiting turned the television on and suddenly started shouting loudly: "The Wall has come down! The Wall has come down!"

Spontaneously, we ran out into the street, jumped into my Renault van and drove off with a roar towards the border. Our first stop was the Oberbaum bridge in Kreuzberg. It was closed and there was no way of crossing there. So we drove on to Moritzplatz, to the Heinestraße border crossing. Here the border was somehow open yet still closed. It was a strange picture which I still cannot really believe today – we played "tag" with the border guards. We pretended to go to the left, so that we could run across the border from the right, and then vice versa. But at some point, we gave up and the guards had won again. Nevertheless, we were determined to cross into East Berlin – straight away. So now we headed for the ultimate target, the Brandenburg Gate, where lots of people were standing on the Wall. Until then, I had not realised that the top of the Wall was wide enough here to accommodate so many people. We too climbed up it and then thought about whether we should jump down on the eastern side. One friend in our group had been deported to the West from a prison in the GDR only five days earlier. He shouted loudly: "I have just got out of there and now I am expected to go back again!?" But, like all the rest of us, he dropped down on the other side. Now I was only a few metres from the Brandenburg Gate. A policeman came straight up to me and asked in a broad Saxon accent: "Where are you going?" I was speechless. He came nearer: "Are you going to our capital city?" I simply said "Yes!" – and the way to the capital city was free. It was like being intoxicated, but without any alcohol. It was a feeling of being completely overwhelmed, a feeling of the greatest possible joy.

Everything that followed, all the celebrations and festivities, did not have anything like the power of that moment – the evening of 9 November 1989 under the Brandenburg Gate ....

MEIN 9. NOVEMBER
MY 9TH NOVEMBER „

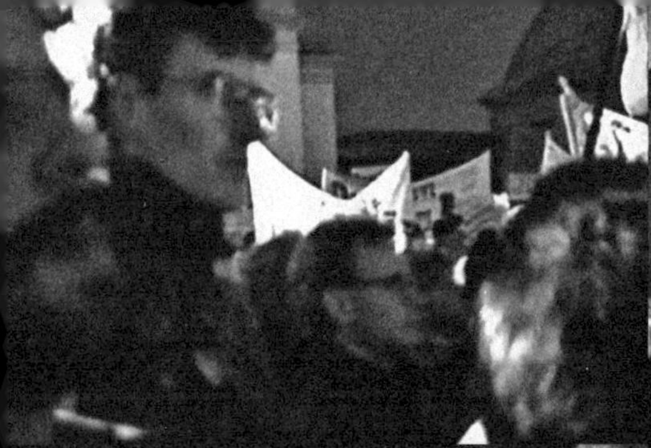
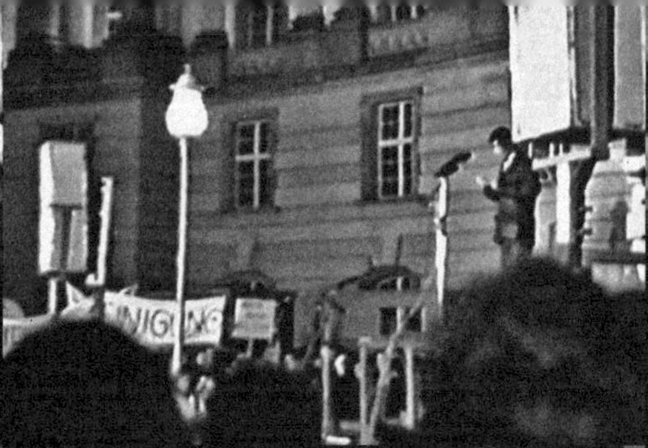
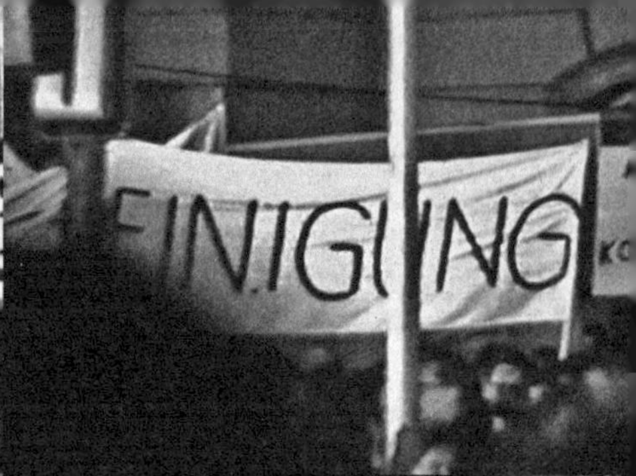
EINIGUNG
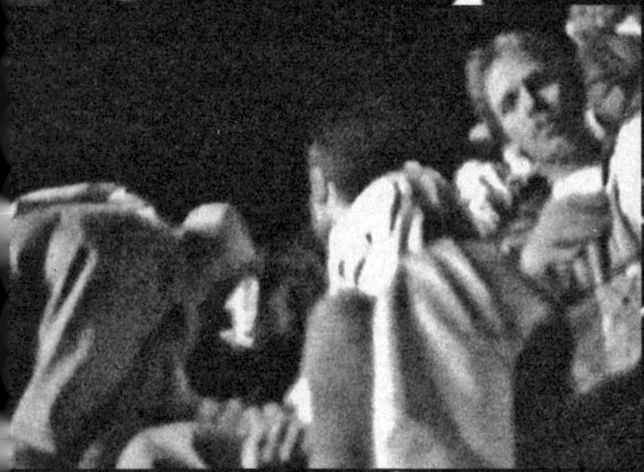
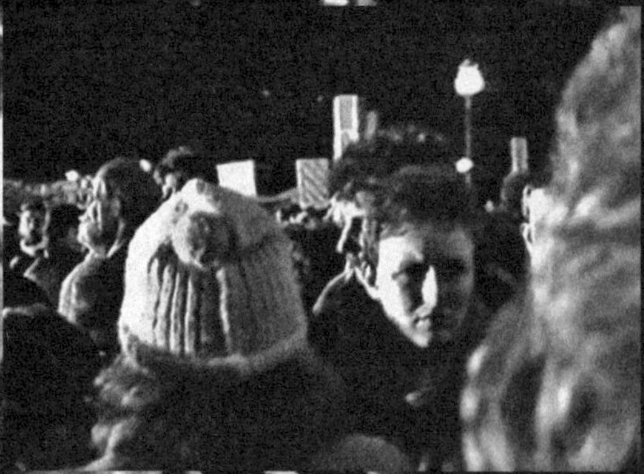
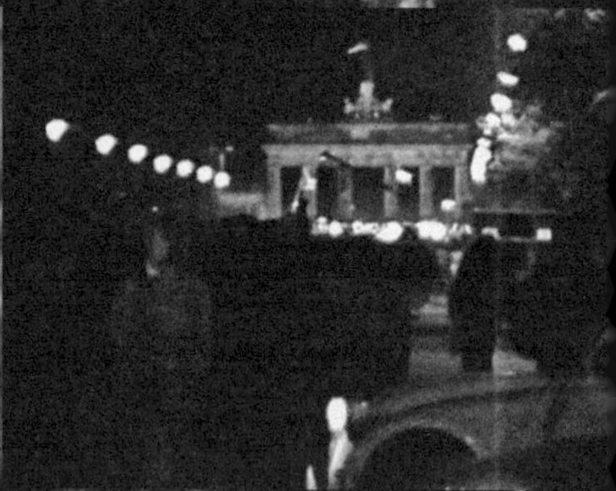
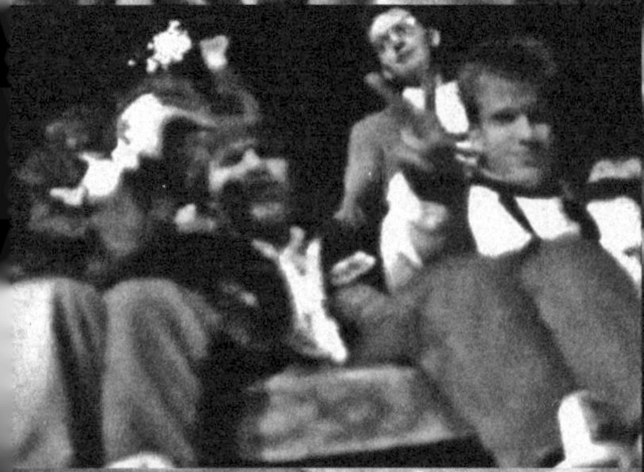
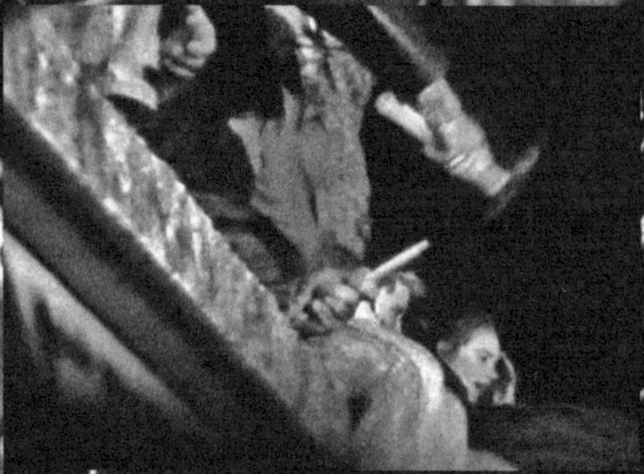
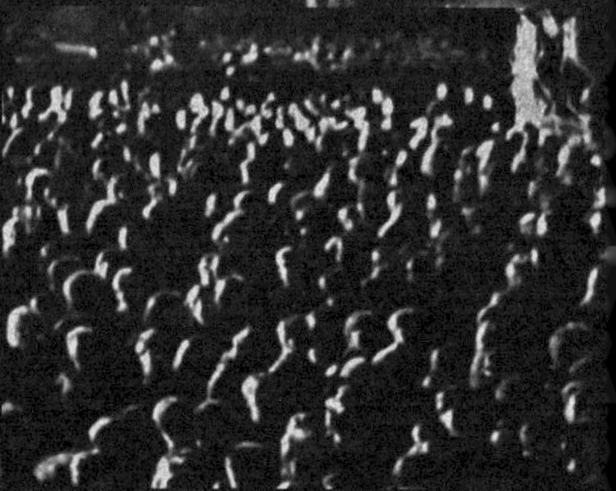
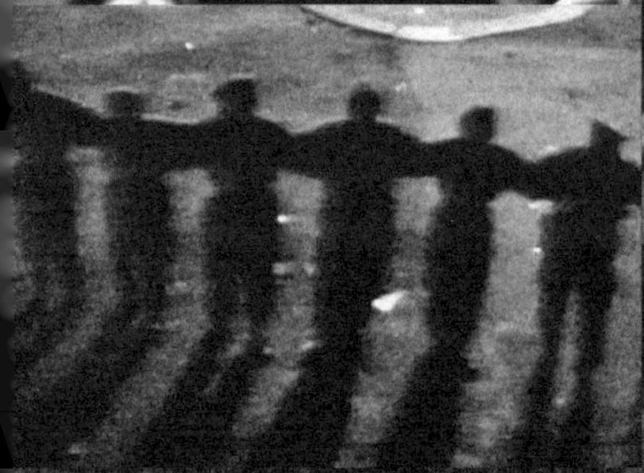
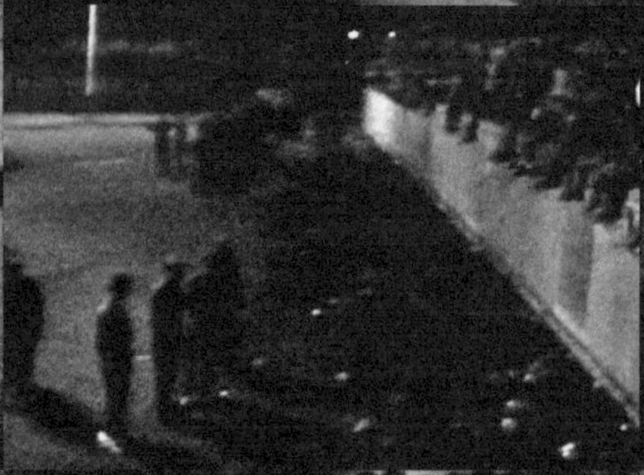
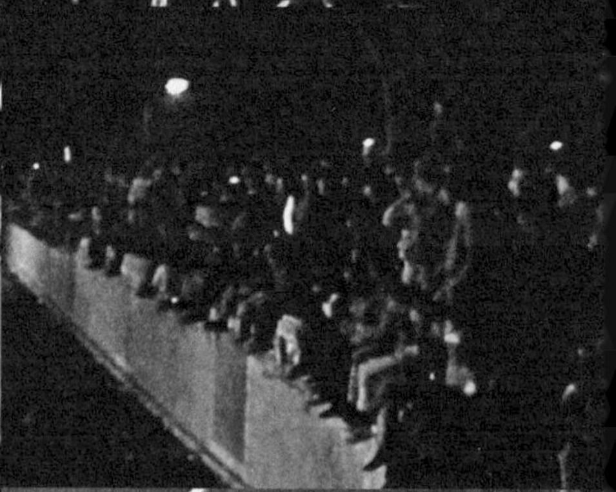
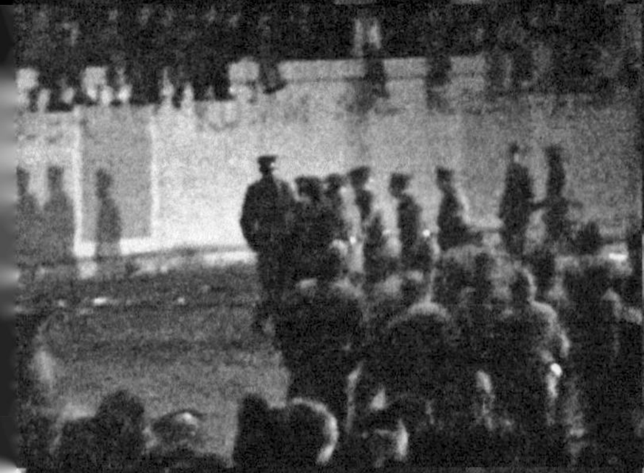

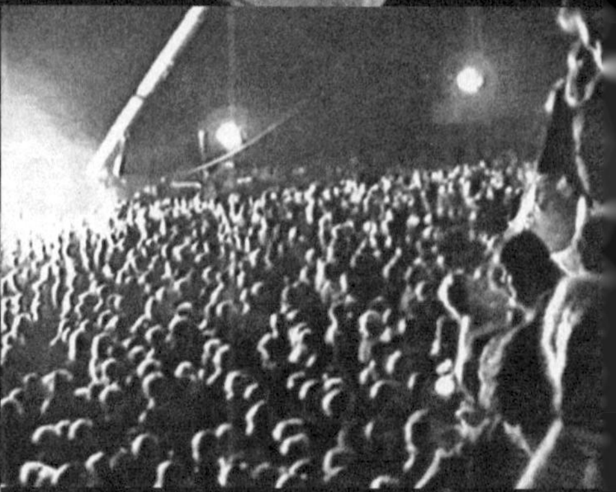
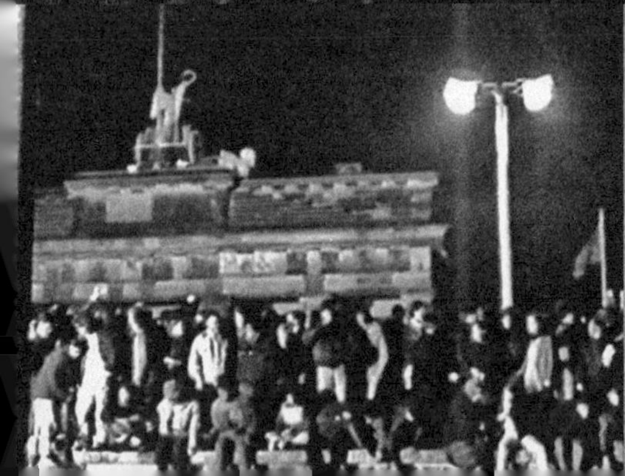
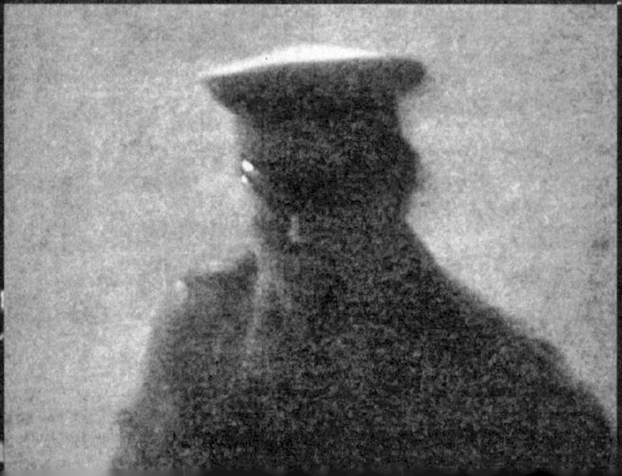
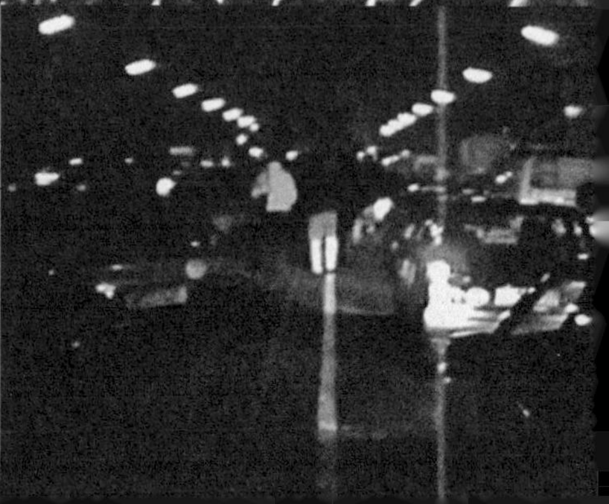

ASISIS FILM DER NACHT ALS DIE MAUER FIEL

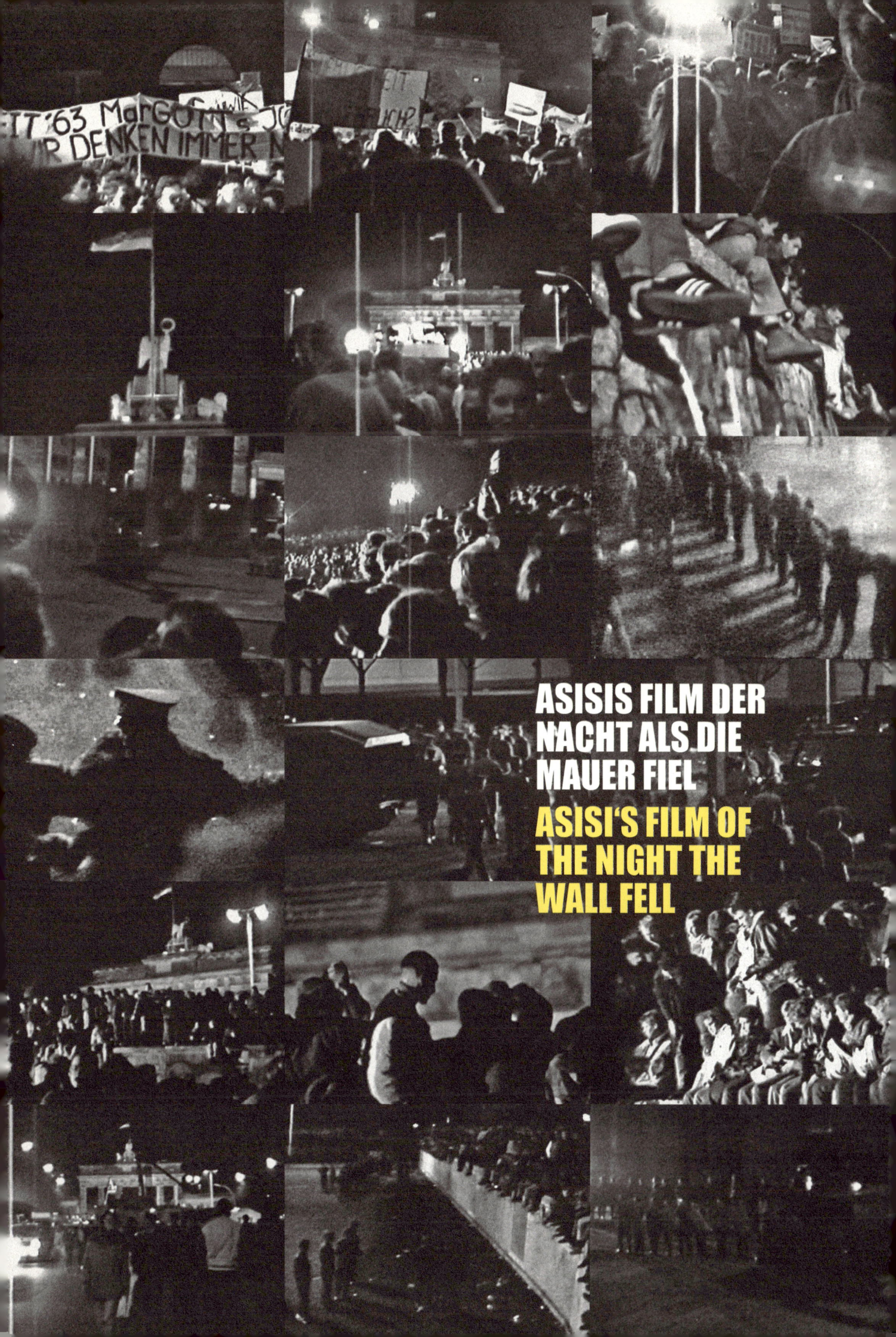

ASISI'S FILM OF THE NIGHT THE WALL FELL

MAUER CHRONOLOGIE
WALL CHRONOLOGY

1961

Zwischen 1949 und 1961 flüchten etwa 2,6 Millionen Menschen aus der DDR in den Westen, ab 1952 überwiegend über Berlin; allein bis zum 13. August 1961 sind es rund 160.000 Flüchtlinge.
Between 1949 and 1961, some 2.6 million people flee to the West from the GDR; from 1952 onwards, this is primarily via Berlin; by 13 August 1961 alone, there were about 160,000 escapees.

15. JUNI JUNE
DDR-Staatsratsvorsitzender Walter Ulbricht erklärt: „Niemand hat die Absicht, eine Mauer zu errichten."
GDR Chairman of the Council of State Walter Ulbricht says: "No-one is planning to build a wall."

13. AUGUST AUGUST
Abriegelung Westberlins und der innerdeutschen Grenze, Baubeginn der Berliner Mauer.
Isolation of West Berlin and the internal German border, start of building of the Berlin Wall.

20. AUGUST AUGUST
Die USA verstärken ihre militärische Präsenz in Berlin um 1500 Soldaten.
The USA increases its military presence in Berlin by another 1500 soldiers.

22. AUGUST AUGUST
Bundeskanzler Konrad Adenauer besucht Westberlin.
West German Chancellor Konrad Adenauer visits West Berlin.

24. AUGUST AUGUST
Der erste Flüchtling wird an der Mauer erschossen.
The first escapee is shot at the Wall.

25. OKTOBER OCTOBER
Panzer der USA und der UdSSR stehen sich in Berlin am alliierten Grenzübergang Checkpoint Charlie gegenüber.
Tanks from the USA and the USSR face each other at Checkpoint Charlie, the Allied border crossing in Berlin.

1962

17. AUGUST AUGUST
Der bei einem Fluchtversuch angeschossene 18jährige Peter Fechter verblutet im Niemandsland.
18-year old Peter Fechter is hit by a bullet while trying to escape and bleeds to death in no man's land.

14.-28. OKTOBER OKTOBER
Die Kuba-Krise zwischen den USA und der Sowjetunion markiert den Wendepunkt in der Geschichte des Kalten Krieges.
The Cuba crisis between the USA and the Soviet Union marks the turning-point in the history of the Cold War.

1963

26. JUNI JUNE
Beim ersten Besuch eines US-Präsidenten nach dem Bau der Mauer drückt John F. Kennedy seine Solidarität mit der eingeschlossenen Bevölkerung von Westberlin aus: „Ich bin ein Berliner!"
On the first visit by a US President after the building of the Wall, John F. Kennedy expresses his solidarity with the entrapped population of West Berlin: "Ish bin ein Bearleener!"

18. DEZEMBER DECEMBER
Das erste Passierscheinabkommen ermöglicht Westberlinern ab 20. Dezember den Verwandtenbesuch im Ostteil der Stadt zu hohen Feiertagen. An der Grenze wird zur Verbesserung der Sicht damit begonnen, einen 100 Meter breiten Geländestreifen zu planieren. Hundelaufanlagen werden eingerichtet.
As of 20 December, the first Travel Permit Agreement enables West Berliners to visit relatives in the eastern section of the city on major public holidays. Work begins on bulldozing a 100-metre wide strip of land on the border to provide a better view. Dog runs are built.

1964

Die DDR führt einen Zwangsumtausch zum Wechselkurs 1:1 für Besucher aus dem westlichen Ausland ein. Der Tagessatz von anfangs fünf D-Mark wird bis 1989 mehrfach erhöht.
The GDR introduces a compulsory currency exchange scheme at a rate of 1:1 for visitors from Western countries. The initial obligatory daily amount of five D-marks is increased several times before 1989.

An der Grenze werden Kraftfahrzeugsperrgräben angelegt und die Wachtürme aus Holz durch Betontürme ersetzt.
Ditches to obstruct motor vehicles are dug at the border and the wooden watchtowers are replaced by concrete towers.

10. SEPTEMBER SEPTEMBER
Rentner aus der DDR dürfen fortan besuchsweise in die Bundesrepublik reisen.
From now on, pensioners from the GDR are permitted to visit West Germany.

5. OKTOBER OCTOBER
Bei einer spektakulären Flucht gelangen 57 Flüchtlinge durch einen elf Meter tiefen und 140 Meter langen Tunnel nach Westberlin.
In a spectacular escape, 57 escapees flee to West Berlin through a tunnel that is 11 metres deep and 140 metres long.

1965

7. APRIL APRIL
Während einer Sitzung des Bundestages in Westberlin überfliegen sowjetische Düsenjäger die Stadt. DDR-Soldaten blockieren die Transitwege nach Westberlin.
During a session of the West German parliament in West Berlin, Soviet jets fly over the city. GDR soldiers block the transit routes to West Berlin.

1967

11. JUNI JUNE
Die DDR führt den Pass- und Visumzwang für Besucher aus dem Westen ein.
The GDR introduces compulsory passports and visas for visitors from the West.

18. AUGUST AUGUST
In einem großangelegten Prozess werden 37 Fluchthelfer in Ostberlin zu langen Haftstrafen verurteilt.
In a large-scale trial, 37 escape helpers are sentenced to long terms of imprisonment in East Berlin.

1968

20./21. AUGUST AUGUST
Der „Prager Frühling" wird durch sowjetisches Militär zerschlagen.
The "Prague Spring" is suppressed by Soviet troops.

1969

28. OKTOBER OCTOBER
Der neue Bundeskanzler Willy Brandt verkündet gegenüber der DDR eine neue Politik unter der Devise „Wandel durch Annäherung".
Willy Brandt, the new West German Chancellor, announces a new policy in dealings with the GDR, using the slogan "Change by Rapprochement".

1971

3. MAI MAY
Nach dem erzwungenen Rücktritt Walter Ulbrichts wird Erich Honecker sein Nachfolger als Erster Sekretär des Zentralkomitees der SED und Vorsitzender des Staatsrates der DDR.
After Walter Ulbricht's forced resignation, he is succeeded by Erich Honecker as General Secretary of the Central Committee of the Socialist Unity Party (SED) and as Chairman of the GDR Council of State.

3. SEPTEMBER SEPTEMBER
Die vier Kriegsalliierten unterzeichnen das „Berlin-Abkommen", das die Sicherheit der Transitwege von Westdeutschland nach Berlin sichert.
The four war Allies sign the "Berlin Agreement" which ensures the safety of the transit routes from West Germany to Berlin.

11. DEZEMBER DECEMBER

Das Transitabkommen zwischen den beiden deutschen Staaten vereinbart pauschale Zahlungen der Bundesrepublik für die Straßennutzung und eine starke Erleichterung der Grenzkontrollen im Transitverkehr durch die DDR.

Agreement made between the two German states provides for flat-rate payments by West Germany for use of roads and a significant easing in the border controls of transit traffic through the GDR.

1972

21. DEZEMBER DECEMBER

Mit dem Grundlagenvertrag zwischen der DDR und der BRD gibt die BRD ihren Alleinvertretungsanspruch auf.

In the Basic Treaty made between the GDR and West Germany, West Germany gives up its claim to sole representation.

1974

14. MÄRZ MARCH

In Bonn und Ostberlin eröffnen „Ständige Vertretungen".

"Permanent legations" are opened in Bonn and East Berlin.

1979

In der DDR wird eine neue „Währung" eingeführt: der Forumscheck. Wer im Intershop einkaufen will, muss seine Devisen zuvor in Forumschecks umtauschen. Um darüber hinaus an harte Währungen zu kommen, erhöht die DDR den Pflichtumtausch für DDR-Besucher aus dem Westen auf 25 DM pro Tag.

A new "currency" is introduced in the GDR, namely the "forum cheque". Anyone wanting to buy in an Intershop must change his foreign currency into "forum cheques" first. To obtain more hard currency, the GDR also increases the obligatory currency exchange rate for Western visitors to the GDR to 25 DM per day.

Die DDR legalisiert im „Gesetz über die Staatsgrenze der Deutschen Demokratischen Republik" den Waffeneinsatz gegen „Grenzverletzer".

In its "Act on the State Frontier of the German Democratic Republic", the GDR legalises the uses of firearms against "frontier trespassers".

1987

6. - 9.JUNI 6TH-9TH JUNE

In Ostberlin versuchen 3000 Rockfans vom Brandenburger Tor aus das Open-Air-Konzert „Rock Salute to Berlin" (u.a. mit Genesis, David Bowie, Eurythmics) vor dem Reichstagsgebäude in Westberlin mitzuhören. Trotz des großen Polizeiaufgebotes fordern die Menschen in der Straße Unter den Linden den Abriss der Mauer und Freiheit, auch Rufe nach Gorbatschow („Gorbi") werden laut.

In East Berlin, 3000 rock fans try to listen from the Brandenburg Gate to the „Rock Salute to Berlin" open-air concert (including Genesis, David Bowie, Eurythmics) held outside the Reichstag building in West Berlin. Despite the large police presence, the people in the road "Unter den Linden" call for the Wall to come down and for freedom; calls for Gorbachev ("Gorbi") are heard.

12. JUNI JUNE

US-Präsident Ronald Reagan fordert vor dem Brandenburger Tor „Mr. Gorbatschow, tear down this wall!"

In front of the Brandenburg Gate, US President Ronald Reagan shouts: "Mr. Gorbachev, tear down this wall!"

17. JUNI JUNE

Aus Anlass des 38. Jahrestages ihrer Gründung beschließt die DDR-Regierung die Abschaffung der Todesstrafe.

On the occasion of the 38th anniversary of its foundation, the government of the GDR decides on the abolition of the death penalty.

26. AUGUST AUGUST

Die Bundesregierung erhöht das Begrüßungsgeld für Besucher aus der DDR von bisher zweimal jährlich 30 DM auf einmal 100 DM pro Besucher und Jahr.

The government of West Germany raises the "welcome money" for visitors from the GDR from 30 DM twice yearly to 100 DM once per visitor and year.

1988

17. JANUAR JANUARY

In Ostberlin hat der Staatssicherheitsdienst rund 120 Angehörige der Friedens- und Menschenrechtsbewegung, die am Rande der traditionellen Luxemburg-Liebknecht-Demonstration für die Freiheit der Andersdenkenden demonstrieren wollen, festgenommen. 54 von ihnen werden zur Ausreise in die Bundesrepublik genötigt.

In East Berlin, State Security (Stasi) arrest some 120 members of the peace and human rights movement who planned to demonstrate for the freedom of dissidents on the fringe of the traditional Luxemburg-Liebknecht demonstration. 54 of them are forced to leave the GDR for West Germany.

14. MÄRZ MARCH

Nach einem Friedensgebet in der Leipziger Nikolaikirche ziehen etwa 300 der etwa 1000 Teilnehmer in einem spontanen Schweigemarsch zur Thomaskirche. Sicherheitskräfte greifen nicht ein.

After prayers for peace in St. Nikolai Church in Leipzig, some 300 of the 1,000 participants join a spontaneous silent march to St. Thomas' Church. Security forces do not intervene.

2. DEZEMBER DECEMBER

Auf einer Tagung des Zentralkomitees der SED lehnt Erich Honecker die sowjetische Reformpolitik von Michail Gorbatschow ab.

At a meeting of the Central Committee of the Socialist Unity Party, Erich Honecker rejects Michael Gorbachev's reform policies.

1989

6. FEBRUAR FEBRUARY

Ein 22jähriger Flüchtling wird das letzte Todesopfer des Schießbefehls an der Berliner Mauer in Berlin.

A 22-year old escapee is the last person to die as a victim of the order to shoot issued to guards at the Berlin Wall.

8. AUGUST AUGUST

Die Ständige Vertretung der Bundesrepublik in Ostberlin wird wegen Überfüllung mit ausreisewilligen DDR-Bürgern geschlossen.

The Permanent Legation of West Germany in East Berlin is closed due to overcrowding by GDR citizens wanting to leave the country.

10./11. SEPTEMBER SEPTEMBER

Ungarn lässt alle dort befindlichen DDR-Flüchtlinge in den Westen ausreisen. Rund 15.000 DDR-Bürger flüchten innerhalb von drei Tagen in die Bundesrepublik.

Hungary allows all the GDR refugees there to travel to the West. Some 15,000 citizens of the GDR flee to West Germany within three days.

30. SEPTEMBER SEPTEMBER

Polen und die CSSR lassen rund 6.000 DDR-Flüchtlinge ausreisen, die sich in den Botschaften der Bundesrepublik in Warschau und Prag aufhalten.

Poland and the CSR allow about 6,000 GDR refugees to leave the country after they have fled to the West German Embassies in Warsaw and Prague.

9. OKTOBER OCTOBER

In Leipzig demonstrieren mehr als 70.000 Menschen für Reformen in der DDR. Es war die entscheidende Demonstration der „Friedlichen Revolution" in der DDR, die zunächst „Dialogbereitschaft" und später die Auflösung der DDR zur Folge hatte.

In Leipzig, more than 70,000 people demonstrate for reforms in the GDR. This was the decisive demonstration in the "peaceful revolution" in the GDR, which led first to "willingness to enter into dialogue" and then the dissolution of the GDR.

6./7. OKTOBER OCTOBER

Die Feierlichkeiten zum 40. Jahrestag der DDR sind begleitet von Unruhen und Protesten. Michail Gorbatschow ist zu Gast und mahnt Reformen an: „Wer zu spät kommt, den bestraft das Leben".

The celebrations to mark the 40th anniversary of the GDR are accompanied by unrest and protest. Michael Gorbachev is a guest and calls for reforms: "Life punishes those who come too late".

18. OKTOBER OCTOBER

Erich Honecker tritt unter Druck als Staatsratsvorsitzender der DDR zurück, sein Nachfolger wird Egon Krenz.

Under pressure, Erich Honecker resigns as Chairman of the Council of State of the GDR; his successor is Egon Krenz.

4. NOVEMBER NOVEMBER

Eine Million Menschen demonstrieren in Ostberlin für Demokratie in der DDR.

One million people demonstrate in East Berlin for democracy in the GDR.

7. NOVEMBER NOVEMBER

Die DDR-Regierung tritt geschlossen zurück.

The whole of the GDR government resigns.

8. NOVEMBER NOVEMBER

Das gesamte SED-Politbüro tritt zurück.

The whole politburo of the Socialist Unity Party (SED) resigns.

9. NOVEMBER NOVEMBER

SED-Politbüromitglied Günter Schabowski verkündet auf einer im DDR-Fernsehen übertragenen Pressekonferenz erhebliche Reiseerleichterungen. Daraufhin passieren noch in derselben Nacht tausende DDR-Bürger in Berlin die Mauer sowie die innerdeutsche Grenze.

At a press conference broadcast on GDR television, Günter Schabowski, a member of the SED politburo, announces substantial easement of travel restrictions. Thereupon, on the same night, thousands of citizens of the GDR cross the Wall in Berlin and the internal German border.

11. NOVEMBER NOVEMBER

Am Potsdamer Platz wird die Mauer eingerissen.

The Wall is broken down on Potsdamer Platz.

23. DEZEMBER DECEMBER

Das Brandenburger Tor in Berlin wird 28 Jahre, zwei Monate und 28 Tage nach dem Bau der Mauer wieder geöffnet.

The Brandenburg Gate in Berlin is re-opened 28 years, 2 months and 28 days after the Wall was built.

SILVESTER NEW YEAR'S EVE

David Hasselhoff singt am Reichstag „Looking for Freedom", obwohl der Text überhaupt nichts mit politischer Freiheit zu tun hat, wird das Lied die missverstandene Vereinigungshymne.

David Hasselhoff sings "Looking for Freedom" by the Reichstag; although the words of the song have nothing whatsoever to do with political freedom, this song becomes the misunderstood hymn of unification.

FAZIT CONCLUSION

Seit dem 13. August 1961 sind an der deutsch-deutschen Grenze, auf der Ostsee und an der Berliner Mauer 765 Menschen bei Fluchtversuchen ums Leben gekommen. In den 28 Jahren, in denen die Mauer stand, sind etwa 40.000 Menschen als „Sperrbrecher" aus der DDR geflohen, indem sie über Mauer und Stacheldraht kletterten, durch Grenzgewässer schwammen oder mit Kleinflugzeugen und selbstgebauten Ballons die Grenze überwanden. Von 1964 bis 1989 kaufte die Bundesrepublik gegen Zahlung von rund 3,4 Milliarden D-Mark etwa 33.000 politische Häftlinge aus der DDR frei.

After 13 August 1961, 765 people died while trying to escape across the inner German border, across the Baltic Sea and across the Berlin Wall. During the 28 years for which the Wall existed, some 40,000 people fled from the GDR as "blockade runners" by climbing over Wall and barbed wire, swimming across frontier waters or crossing the border in small aircraft and homemade air balloons. Between 1964 and 1989, West Germany paid some 3.4 billion DM to free about 33,000 political prisoners from the GDR.

DIE MAUER IN ZAHLEN
THE WALL IN FIGURES

GRENZE BORDER

ZWISCHEN OST- UND WESTBERLIN
BETWEEN EAST AND WEST BERLIN

155KM GESAMTLÄNGE / TOTAL LENGTH

112KM AUSSENRING / OUTER RING

43KM INNERSTÄDTISCH / INNER-CITY

105,5KM
KRAFTFAHRZEUG-SPERRGRÄBEN
MOTOR VEHICLE BLOCKING DITCHES

127,5KM
KONTAKT- BZW. SIGNALZÄUNE
CONTACT OR SIGNAL FENCES

124,3KM
KOLONNENWEG
CONVOY ROAD

259 HUNDELAUFANLAGEN / DOG RUNS

20 BUNKER / BUNKERS

302 BEOBACHTUNGSTÜRME / OBSERVATION TOWERS

Legend

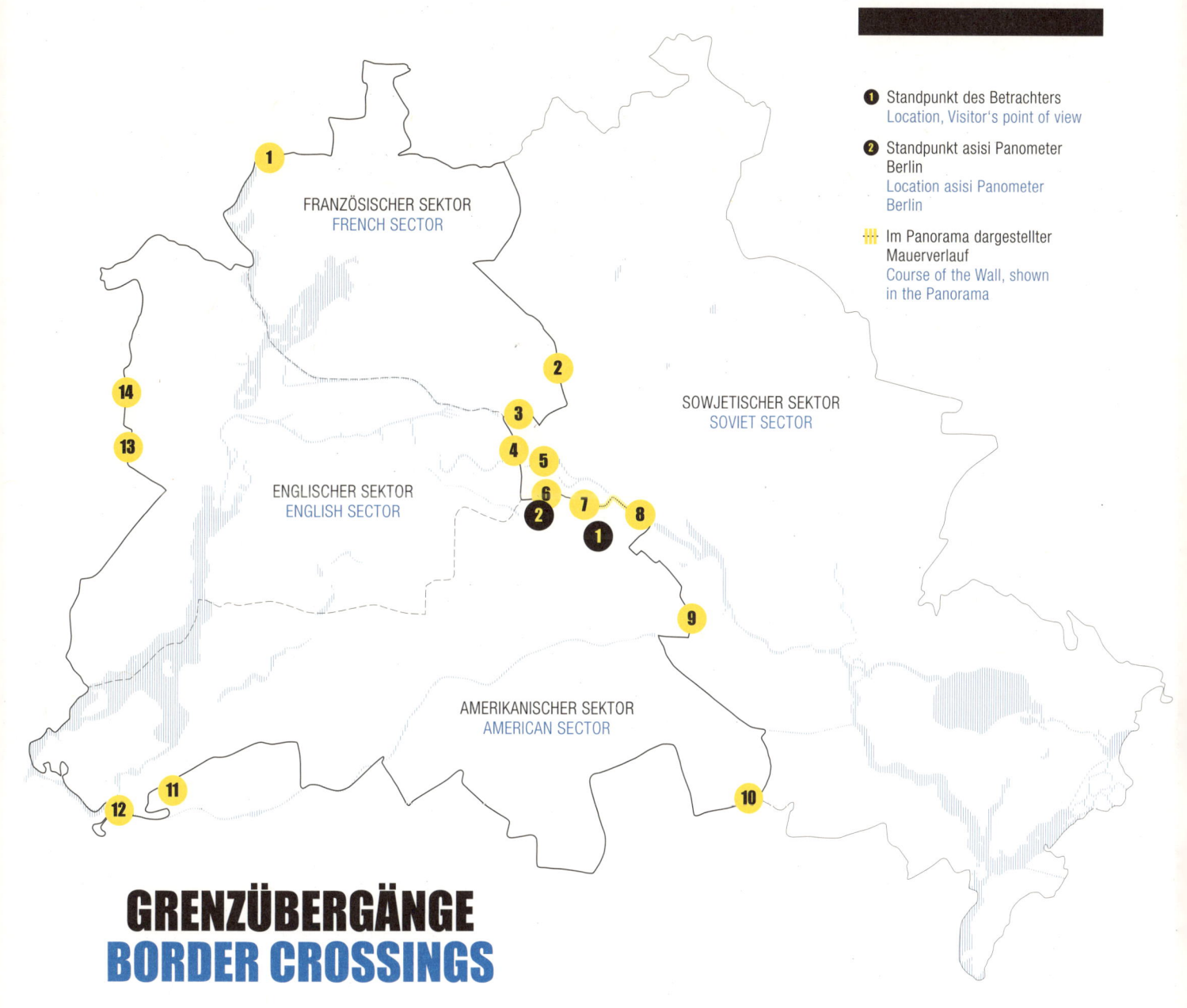

- **1** Standpunkt des Betrachters
  Location, Visitor's point of view
- **2** Standpunkt asisi Panometer Berlin
  Location asisi Panometer Berlin
- ||| Im Panorama dargestellter Mauerverlauf
  Course of the Wall, shown in the Panorama

FRANZÖSISCHER SEKTOR
FRENCH SECTOR

SOWJETISCHER SEKTOR
SOVIET SECTOR

ENGLISCHER SEKTOR
ENGLISH SECTOR

AMERIKANISCHER SEKTOR
AMERICAN SECTOR

GRENZÜBERGÄNGE
BORDER CROSSINGS

8 ZWISCHEN OST- UND WESTBERLIN (STRASSE/SCHIENE)
BETWEEN EAST AND WEST BERLIN (ROAD/RAIL)

6 ZWISCHEN DER DDR UND WESTBERLIN (STRASSE/SCHIENE)
BETWEEN GDR AND WEST BERLIN (ROAD/RAIL)

1. Stolpe/Heiligensee
   (nur Transit)
   (only Transit)
2. Bornholmer Straße/Bösebrücke
   (nur Westberliner und Bürger der BRD)
   (only West Berliners and citizens of West Germany (FRG))
3. Chauseestraße/Reinickendorfer Straße
   (nur Westberliner)
   (only West Berliners)
4. Invalidenstraße/Sandkrugbrücke
   (nur Westberliner)
   (only West Berliners)
5. Bahnhof Friedrichstraße
   Train station Friedrichstraße
6. Checkpoint Charlie/Friedrichstraße
   (nur ausländische Diplomaten)
   (only foreign diplomates)
7. Heinrich-Heine Straße/Prinzenstraße
   (nur Bürger der BRD)
   (only citizens of the FRG)
8. Oberbaumbrücke
   (nur Westberliner)
   (only West Berliners)
9. Sonnenallee
   (nur Westberliner)
   (only West Berliners)
10. Waltersdorfer Chaussee
    (nur Westberliner, Ausländer nur zum Flughafen Schönefeld)
    (only West Berliners, foreigners only to the airport)
11. Dreilinden/Drewitz
    (nur Transit)
    (only Transit)
12. Griebnitzsee/Wannsee
    (nur Bahntransit)
    (only train transit)
13. Heerstraße
14. Staaken/Spandau
    (nur Bahntransit)
    (only train transit)

THE MAKING OF

asisi
Sandra
DIE MAUER
TICKETS TICKET COUNTE
EINGANG
ENTRY

ROM 312 ROME 312

ASISI PANOMETER DRESDEN
BIS 18. NOVEMBER 2012
UNTIL 18 NOVEMBER 2012

DAS ERLEBNIS DER ANTIKEN WELTSTADT

Das ROM – Panorama zeigt die prächtigste Kapitale der Antike im Jahr 312 n. Chr. Der Besucher erlebt Kaiser Konstantin, der seinen Gegner Maxentius besiegt hat und nun als alleiniger Herrscher mit seinem Gefolge in die Millionenstadt einzieht. Von der fünfzehn Meter hohen Besucherplattform öffnet das 360°-Panorama den Blick weit über die Metropole hinaus. Über ihre Tempel, Paläste, Thermen, Basiliken und Mietskasernen hinweg bis hin zu den Albaner Bergen am Horizont. Vorlage für Yadegar Asisi war ein historisches Panorama aus dem Jahr 1889.

Für Asisi ist es ein persönliches Highlight, in Dresden sein Antikenpanorama ROM 312 zeitgleich zum Antikenpanorama PERGAMON in Berlin zu zeigen. So schlägt ROM 312 noch bis 18. November 2012 eine einzigartige Brücke von der römischen zur griechischen Antike.

EXPERIENCE THE ANCIENT CAPITAL OF THE WORLD

The ROME 312 panorama shows the most magnificent capitals of antiquity in the year 312 CE. Visitors can witness Emperor Constantine entering the large city of over one million inhabitants with his entourage and legionaries as the sole ruler after the defeat of his opponent Maxentius. From the fifteen-meter high viewing platform, the 360° panorama offers a view over and beyond the metropolis, across its temples, palaces, thermal baths, basilicas and tenements to the Albanian mountains on the horizon. Yadegar Asisi's model for this work was a historical panorama from the year 1889.

It is a personal highlight for Asisi to be able to show his panorama ROME 312 in Dresden at the same time as the exhibition of his panorama PERGAMON in Berlin. Running until 18th November 2012, ROME 312 will create a bridge between the two cities of Roman and Greek antiquity.

DRESDEN DRESDEN

ASISI PANOMETER DRESDEN
AB 1. DEZEMBER 2012
FROM 1 DECEMBER 2012

MYTHOS DER BAROCKEN RESIDENZSTADT

Yadegar Asisi legt in seinem 360°-Panorama über die barocke Glanzzeit Dresdens den Fokus auf das Leben am sächsischen Hofe und das Alltagsleben der Bürger, Krämer, Fischer, Dienstboten und Handwerker. Er verdichtet die Zeit von etwa 1695 bis 1760 zu einer künstlerischen Momentaufnahme des Dresdner Barocks.

Den „Geruch der Zeit" atmen förmlich die Szenen mit den historischen Personen im Rundbild. So sieht man Zar Peter I., den Erfinder des Porzellans Böttger, Johann Sebastian Bach oder den Hofnarr Joseph Fröhlich. Zu sehen ist auch die Ankunft der Sixtinischen Madonna im Jahr 1754. Vergessene Alltagsepisoden mit Holztreidlern und Waschfrauen an der Elbe, Sänftenträgern und Komödianten auf den Plätzen und vielem mehr, machen das Panorama zu einem erlebbaren Kunstraum dieser Epoche. Auch die Nachtvariante hält glanzvolle Eindrücke bereit.

MYTH OF THE BAROQUE ROYAL SEAT

Yadegar Asisi's 360° panorama of the glorious Baroque period in Dresden focuses on life in the Saxon court as well as the daily lives of citizens, merchants, fishermen, servants and tradesmen. Asisi condenses the period from about 1695 to 1760 into an artistic snapshot of Dresden Baroque.

The scenes with historical persons capture the „scent of the age". Here we can see Tsar Peter I, the European discoverer of porcelain, Böttger, Johann Sebastian Bach and the court jester Joseph Fröhlich. We also witness the arrival of the Sistine Madonna in the year 1754. Forgotten episodes from daily life with barge-towspulling shipments of wood and washerwomen at work on the banks of the river Elbe, litter bearers and comedians in the town squares and many other details turn this panoramic picture into a three-dimensional space that brings this era to life. The simulation of the city at night adds a stunning finishing touch to the experience.

AMAZONIEN AMAZONIA

**ASISI PANOMETER LEIPZIG
BIS 6. JANUAR 2013
UNTIL 6 JANUARY 2013**

YADEGAR ASISIS ZAUBERBILD DER NATUR

Yadegar Asisi führt uns mit seinem Panorama AMAZONIEN auf eine faszinierende Erkundungstour in die südamerikanischen Tropen. Und das mitten in Leipzig. Die Besucher erleben in dem 3.200 Quadratmeter großen Riesenrundbild die faszinierende Schönheit Amazoniens. Aus sechs Metern Höhe öffnet sich wie auf einer Lichtung der Blick weit in die Tiefen des Regenwaldes. Mit einem Fernglas lassen sich Schmetterlinge, Papageien oder ein versteckter Jaguar im Geäst der tropischen Baumriesen entdecken.

Das weltgrößte 360°-Panorama hat Yadegar Asisi als Hommage an Alexander von Humboldt konzipiert. Die Komplexität des Ökosystems Regenwald wird durch eine Tag- und Nachtsimulation mit Sonnenauf- und -untergang, prasselnden Regen und die tiefdunkle Nacht der Tropen mit ihren unzähligen Geräuschen für den Besucher erlebbar.

YADEGAR ASISIS MAGICAL PICTURE OF NATURE

Yadegar Asisi whisks us on a fascinating discovery of the South American tropics in his panorama AMAZONIA. And that in the heart of Leipzig! Visitors can experience the fascinating beauty of the Amazon in the 3,200 square metre panorama. At a height of six meters, it seems as if we are looking into a clearing, deep in the forest as it stretches out before us. With the help of binoculars, it is possible to discover butterflies, parrots and a jaguar lurking in the branches of the giant, tropical trees.

The world's largest 360° panorama, AMAZONIA was conceived by Yadegar Asisi as a homage to Alexander von Humboldt. The complexity of the ecosystem of the rainforest is brought to life through a simulation of night and day with sunrise and sunset, rain showers and the pitch dark of a tropical night with its multitude of sounds and noises.

EVEREST EVEREST

**ASISI PANOMETER LEIPZIG
AB 12. JANUAR 2013
FROM 12 JANUARY 2013**

ERLEBNIS ZWISCHEN EXPEDITION UND TRADITION

Vom letzten Basislager vor dem Gipfel des Mount Everest erhebt sich die majestätische Bergwelt und die der ihn umgebenden Achttausender. Ähnlich sieht man es auch von der sechs Meter hohen Besucherplattform inmitten des Panoramas. Von Hellblau bis Aquamarin, von Schneeweiß bis zu Schwarz erschließt sich die Hochgebirgswelt in 6000 bis 8848 Meter Höhe.

Buddhistisch-tibetanische Elemente, wie etwa ein Sand-Mandala, Schreine, Stupas, Rollbilder und Gebetsfahnen vermitteln die kontrastierende fernöstliche Sicht auf den Everest. Neben der Tagsequenz bietet vor allem die Nachtsequenz mit ihrer mondbeschienenen Eiswelt eine ganz eigene magische Stimmung.

EXPERIENCE BETWEEN EXPEDITION AND TRADITION

The majestic mountain landscape and the towering eight-thousander rise up from the last base camp before the final ascent to the summit of Mount Everest. The six-meter high viewing platform in the centre of the panoramic picture allows visitors to view the mountain from a similar perspective. With colours ranging from light blue to aquamarine, snow white to deep black, this mountainous world at a height of 6000 to 8848 metres above sea level unfolds before our eyes.

Tibetan Buddhist objects such as a sand mandala, shrines, stupas, scroll paintings and prayer flags convey the contrasting attitude of Eastern cultures towards Mount Everest. As well as the daytime simulation, visitors can also experience the magical atmosphere of this icy world at night time, with the snowy mountains glistening in the moonlight.

BILDNACHWEIS
PICTURE CREDITS

Seite Page 08-09
Yadegar Asisis Pantomime Film „Freiheit",
1980, Iranisches Fernsehen
Yadegar Asisi's pantomime film „Freedom",
1980, Iranian Television
© asisi

Seite Page 12-13
© asisi

Seite Page 16
Landesarchiv Berlin, F Rep. 290, Not. 1 G
Kreuzberg, Nr. 259849 / W. Albrecht

Seite Page 19-22
© asisi

Seite Page 25
© asisi

Seite Page 26
1 Bundesregierung, B 145 Bild-00018905, Gert Schütz, 25. März 1967
2 © asisi
3 Bundesregierung, B 145 Bild-00019605, Gert Schütz, 23. Dezember 1962

Seite Page 28
© Berliner Unterwelten e.V. / Sammlung Klaus Köppen

Seite Page 31
1 © Axel Springer AG
2 Landesarchiv Berlin, F Rep. 290, Not. 1 G, Nr. 93957 / Karl-Heinz Schubert

Seite Page 33
1 Landesarchiv Berlin, F Rep. 290, Not. 1 G, Nr. 76482/ Horst Siegmann
2 © Werner Zellien / www.wernerzellien.com
3 © ddpimages/ AP/ Werner Kreusch

Seite Page 35
1 Landesarchiv Berlin, F Rep. 290, Not. 1 G, Nr. 309087/ Edmund Kasperski
2 ©asisi

Seite Page 36
1 Presse- und Informationsamt der Bundesregierung, Scgütz
2 © asisi
3 © asisi

Seite Page 38
© Deutschlandradio

Seite Page 39-40
1 Landesarchiv Berlin, F Rep. 290, Not. 1 G, Nr. 78067 / Horst Siegmann
2 Landesarchiv Berlin, F Rep. 290, Not. 1 G, Nr. 88454 / H. Bier
3 Landesarchiv Berlin, F Rep. 290, Not. 1 G, Nr. 85520 / Gert Schütz
4 Landesarchiv Berlin, F Rep. 290, Not. 1 G / Johann Willa

Seite Page 42-43
1 © asisi
2 Bundesarchiv, Bild 183-H1003-0001-049, Horst Sturm, 3. Oktober 1969
3 Bundesarchiv, Bild 183-G1007-0036-001, Siegfried Voigt, 7. Oktober 1968
4 Bundesarchiv, Bild 183-E0321-0012-002, Joachim Spremberg, 21. März 1966
5 Bundesarchiv, Bild 183-E0623-0009-002, Joachim Spremberg, 23. Juni 1966

Seite Page 44
1 © asisi
2 © asisi

Seite Page 47
1 © Peter Homann/bsd-photo-archiv
2 © Peter Homann/bsd-photo-archiv
3 © Peter Homann/bsd-photo-archiv

Seite Page 49
1 © asisi
2 Bundesregierung, B 145 Bild-00049135, Klaus Lehnartz, 1.Mai 1989
3 © asisi

Seite Page 51
© Robert Conrad / www.lumabytes.com

Seite Page 52
1 © asisi
2 © Robert Conrad / www.lumabytes.com

Seite Page 55
1 © Hendrik Gerrit Pastor / mauerfotos-hendrikpastor.de
2 © asisi

Seite Page 56-57
1 © asisi
2 © Karin Kiehn
3 © asisi
4 © asisi

Seite Page 59
1 © asisi
2 © asisi
3 © Peter Homann/bsd-photo-archiv

Seite Page 60
1 Bundesregierung, B 145 Bild-00004009, Engelbert Reineke, 11. Juni 1982
2 © Peter Homann/bsd-photo-archiv

Seite Page 62-63
Yadegar Asisis Pantomime Film „Freiheit", 1980, Iranisches Fernsehen
Yadegar Asisi's pantomime film „Freedom", 1980, Iranian Television
© asisi

Seite Page 64-65
© asisi

Seite Page 70-71
© asisi / Tom Schulze

IMPRESSUM
IMPRINT

1. AUFLAGE 2012
1ST EDITION 2012
© 2012 asisi Edition
Alle Rechte vorbehalten.
All rights reserved

HERAUSGEBER PUBLISHED BY
asisi GmbH
Oranienplatz 2
10999 Berlin
T +49(0)30.6 95 80 86-0
office@asisi.de
www.asisi.de

TEXTE TEXTS
Yadegar Asisi
Dr. Stephan Oettermann
Prof. Dr. Hope M. Harisson

LEKTORAT EDITING
Kathrin Francik
Ulla Heise

KORREKTORAT CORRECTION
Karsten Grebe
Ulrike Pötzsch
Stephan Oettermann

ÜBERSETZUNG INS ENGLISCHE
TRANSLATION INTO ENGLISH
Julia Grünschläger-Sutton
für Übersetzungsbüro Macklin GmbH

ART DIRECTION
Mathias Thiel

GESTALTUNG/SATZ DESIGN/LAYOUT
Sandra Knüpfer

KOORDINATION CO-ORDINATION
Denise Lüderitz

BILDREDAKTION PICTURE EDITOR
Maria Mouratidou

GRAFIKEN GRAPHIC WORK
Sandra Knüpfer
Malte Koslowski,
Dona Assisi
Denise Lüderitz

DRUCK PRINTING
Druckhaus Berlin-Mitte GmbH

PAPIER PAPER
Maschinengraupappe (Umschlag)
RecyStar Polar (Inhalt)

ISBN 978-3-00-037202-5

TEAM ASISI

PANORAMABILD
PANORAMA PICTURE

KÜNSTLER ARTISTS
Yadegar Asisi mit with
Alexander Assisi

MITARBEIT ASSISTANCE
Dona Assisi

3D MODELING
Matthias Meye
Reto Assisi

KURATOR CURATOR
Dr. Stephan Oettermann

SOUNDDESIGN, TONCOLLAGE UND MISCHUNG
SOUND DESIGN, SOUND COLLAGE AND MIXING
Eric Babak

RECHERCHE/ASSISTENZ
RESEARCH/ASSISTANCE
Mir Nezam Madani

ARCHITEKTUR UND AUSSTELLUNG
ARCHITECTURE AND EXHIBITION

KÜNSTLERISCHE LEITUNG
ART MANAGEMENT
Yadegar Asisi

ART DIRECTOR
Mathias Thiel

KOORDINATION ARCHITEKTUR
ARCHITECTURAL CO-ORDINATION
Nick Haseloff

MITARBEIT ASSISTANCE
Malte Koslowski
Matthias Meye
Kaj Knüpfer

KOMMUNIKATION
COMMUNICATION

PUBLIC RELATIONS
Karsten Grebe

MARKETING
Irina Schotte

ÖFFENTLICHKEITSARBEIT/SOCIAL MEDIA
PUBLIC RELATIONS WORK/SOCIAL MEDIA
Ulrike Pötzsch

VERTRIEB SALES
Angelika Taudien

PÄDAGOGIK EDUCATION
Markku Weber

LIZENZEN UND KOMMUNIKATION
LICENCES AND COMMUNICATION
Maria Mouratidou

GRAFIK
GRAPHIC WORK

GRAFIK UND KOORDINATION
GRAPHIC WORK AND CO-ORDINATION
Denise Lüderitz

ENTWURF DESIGN
Sandra Knüpfer

BACKOFFICE

FINANZEN UND BETRIEBSORGANISATION
FINANCES AND BUSINESS ORGANISATION
Carola Ohmann
Dominik Bolender

SEKRETARIAT
SECRETARIAT
Gabi Dressler

IT-KOORDINATION IT CO-ORDINATION
Wolfram Schanze

BESUCHERSERVICE
VISITOR SERVICE

Stefanie Schubert
Elsa Midekke
Alexander Wolsza

TEAM – ASISI PANOMETER LEIPZIG

Nadine Sagolla
Thomas Sklarek
André Porzig
Ines Müller
Petra Först
Norbert Jonek

TEAM – ASISI PANOMETER DRESDEN

Helena Kornilow
Jana Schuh
Nicole Kunz
Günther Knecht

BAU
CONSTRUCTION

ENTWURF DESIGN
asisi GmbH

PLANUNG UND AUSFÜHRUNG
PLANNING AND EXECUTION
Behzadi + Partner Architekten BDA
Generalplanung, Berlin

LEINWANDDRUCK SCREEN PRINTING
Marx & Moschner GmbH, Lennestadt

GRUNDSTÜCKSVERWALTUNG PROPERTY MANAGEMENT
Rechtsanwälte Schwemer Titz & Tötter, Berlin

STATIK STRUCTURAL ANALYSIS
Ingenieurbüro Baumann, Zwickau;
Beratende Ingenieure Dierks, Babilon und Voigt,
Berlin; Ingenieurbüro Frankhänel & Müller,
Leipzig

PRÜFSTATIK STRUCTURAL CALCULATION
Krebs & Kiefer, Beratende Ingenieure für das
Bauwesen GmbH, Berlin

BRANDSCHUTZ FIRE PREVENTION CHECK
Ingenieurbüro für Brandschutz Thomas Böhme,
Leipzig

BRANDSCHUTZPRÜFUNG FIRE PREVENTION CHECK
Prüfingenieure Steglich & Schuhmann GbR,
Leipzig

HLS-PLANUNG
HEATING, LIGHTING AND SANITARY PLANNING
IKL + Partner Ingenieurgesellschaft mbH, Berlin

BAUGRUNDGUTACHTEN FOUNDATIONS REPORT
MKP, Prof. Dr.-Ing. H. Müller-Kirchenbauer u.
Partner GmbH, Berlin

SCHALLSCHUTZ SOUND INSULATION
MFPA Leipzig GmbH, Leipzig

STATIK PANORAMA
STRUCTURAL ANALYSIS OF PANORAMA
BfL_Tritthard u. Richter, Radolfzell

STAHLBAU ROTUNDE
STEEL CONSTRUCTION OF ROTUNDA
Metallbau Hausmann GmbH, Kleinthiemig

LICHT- & SOUNDTECHNIK LIGHT- & SOUNDTECHNIK
Frontsound Veranstaltungstechnik GbR, Leipzig

ELEKTRO ELEKTRO
SKS Elektrotechnik GmbH, Leipzig

ZIMMEREI UND AUSBAU CARPENTRY AND FITTINGS
Frame-Work, Berlin

TISCHLER TISCHLER
Tischlerei Diedrich, Leipzig

PANORAMAHÖHENARBEITEN
PANORAMA HEIGHT WORK
Gerriets GmbH, Umkirch
Jan Fehling GmbH, Berlin

ELEKTRO ELECTRICAL WORK
SKS Elektrotechnik GmbH, Leipzig

TIEF-ROHBAUARBEITEN
UNDERGROUND PRELIMINARY WORK
Kasimir Bauunternehmung GmbH, Berlin

GERÜSTBAU SCAFFOLDING
Gerüstbau Tisch GmbH Berlin, Berlin

Das Magazin, das schlauer macht.

Alle zwei Monate neu.

Über 30 % sparen – HÖRZU WISSEN im Abo

Jetzt 3 Hefte für nur 7 € bestellen: 01805-012293*

*0,14 €/Min. aus dem dt. Festnetz (max. 0,42 €/Min. aus dem Mobilfunknetz)

DAS VOLLE PROGRAMM
LEIDENSCHAFT

rbb FERNSEHEN

RBB-ONLINE.DE